Beauty Is *O*xygen

Michael —
Thanks for all your support,
and your love for beauty!
— Wes

Beauty Is *O*xygen

Finding a Faith That Breathes

Wesley Vander Lugt

WILLIAM B. EERDMANS PUBLISHING COMPANY
GRAND RAPIDS, MICHIGAN

Wm. B. Eerdmans Publishing Co.
4035 Park East Court SE, Grand Rapids, Michigan 49546
www.eerdmans.com

Book design by Lydia Hall

Printed in the United States of America

30 29 28 27 26 25 24   1 2 3 4 5 6 7

ISBN 978-0-8028-8325-4

Library of Congress Cataloging-in-Publication Data

A catalog record for this book is available from the Library
of Congress.

*In loving memory of Stonewood Acres
and all the ways God's beauty goes
belonging there*

Contents

CONTENTS

Foreword

Everyone has an opinion on beauty. At what age do we become defensive of our opinions on what is beautiful and what is not? Genesis confirms that our ability to perceive beauty existed before conflict and strife entered the world. A tree ignited veneration. Later, the tree's beautiful fruit was the vehicle for humankind's downfall. But the thief shall not blame the jewel's allure for thievery.

Beauty is not the problem.

Our efforts to water the seeds of beauty will sprout both the waterlily and the weed. A passionate homily can awaken a tender tear in a soul. That same homily can also stoke curious concerns. Like beauty, those who label her are unfixed variables hoping to be settled once our dim mirrors are cleaned.

As this book explores, beauty is a tapestry woven with both charming and harmful threads due to our subjective taste, affinities, and *malaise*. Beauty can foster connection and community while enabling us to share our passions and perspectives, creating a sense of unity in appreciation. It can also sow seeds of division, as what is beautiful to one might be inconsequential or even unattractive to another. This diversity of perception often leads to bad evaluations and societal standards that could exclude certain expressions of beauty, selling inadequacy, inferiority, or envy.

Consequently, the way we communicate about beauty should embrace the multiplicity of perspectives and expressions, celebrating differences while being mindful of the potential for exclusion or judgment that our subjective preferences can inadvertently create. We must not forget our mirrors are dim.

I believe this book will do the redemptive work of clearing off some of the human smudge we've placed on our dim mirrors. Dr. Vander Lugt rightly states our need for beauty and how to discern it through godly frames. Beauty can settle in the auditorium of high art and on the porches where folklore is passed. Beauty is needed in times of trauma, celebration, and indifference.

Let us never grow tired of speaking about beauty. Let us grow wiser in how we evaluate it. Let us find beauty in what many might call the ordinary. Furthermore, let us inspect our hearts for why it is no longer captivating. Let us understand that, like oxygen, there is no scarcity of beauty. It's a currency that all can use. Let the refrains and rhythms of this book help you to inhale the beauty around us. Breathe and meditate on the limitations in our knowing, hearing, and seeing.

The novelist Haruki Murakami details how two men have two different ways of "inhaling" the beauty of a magnificent mountain. One man finds fulfillment with his distant observation while the other finds fulfillment only in his ability to ascend it.[1] Let us learn to appreciate the diversity in the consumption and curation of beauty. Furthermore, as Dr. Vander Lugt urges, let us have a redeemed and grace-centered view of beauty. As people who are forgiven much, we have a charitable posture in our evaluation. We know true beauty because we know true corruption. We who once confessed to having vile and ugly souls could be shining examples of knowing redemptive beauty.

Dr. Vander Lugt also reminds us that beauty and tragedy can coexist. The things we can perceive as terrifying and tragic can also be beautiful. Salvation is the most complex demonstration of Yahweh's spangled display of beauty. Good Friday can only be called good if a terrifying and tragic event had a great reward on the other side of that humiliating act. For that act we shout, "Hallelujah!" This tragedy is made beautiful.

There will be a time when we need no assistance on how to discover beauty. No assistance on how to display it. We shall not grow bored even given its ubiquity. Our mirrors will no longer be dim. In the meantime, beauty in all its complexity is oxygen. Let this book teach you how to breathe deeply.

Sho Baraka

INTRODUCTION

Why Beauty Matters

I tried to start writing this book many times, but it's difficult to find fitting words to describe the power, ubiquity, and necessity of beauty. However inadequate the words may be, I kept coming back to the notion that *beauty is oxygen* for a living, breathing faith. In sharing with people about this writing project, reactions have ranged from deep resonance to critical resistance. Wherever you find yourself on that spectrum: welcome! If you're reading from a place of resonance, I hope this book will provide language and rationale for your own powerful experiences of beauty. If you're reading from a place of resistance, perhaps wondering if writing about beauty is a fool's errand, I hope you'll be pleasantly surprised and gently challenged by the reasonableness of this project. My goal, however, is not to make beauty reasonable but to allow it to remain mysterious and therefore something that can generate wonder, shape our lives, and elicit our worship. As G. K. Chesterton wrote, "The morbid logician seeks to make everything lucid, and succeeds in making everything mysterious. The mystic allows one thing to be mysterious, and everything becomes lucid."[1]

As with most mysteries, thinking about beauty brings us into deep and often choppy waters. The concept of beauty has been abused and misused in all sorts of philosophical, theological, ethical, social, and cultural ways.[2] Beauty has been limited by narrow categories (proportion, harmony, symmetry), reduced to personal preference ("beauty is in the eye of the beholder"), linked with particular forms of so-called high art (as opposed to "popular" or "folk" art) claimed as the purview of a privileged class (the people who can access and afford "high art"), disassociated from its function in everyday life ("art for art's sake"), attached to certain kinds of bodies (skinny, proportionate, white), leveraged for oppressive agendas (racialized, colonial aesthetics), reduced to whatever produces pleasant feelings (like the sentimentality of Christian kitsch), and utilized to sell products and line pockets (especially within capitalist economies). It's a fraught history, and for these reasons and others some contemporary artists and thinkers have abandoned beauty as a description or goal of their work.[3]

So why keep talking about beauty? Quite simply, because the presence of beauty persists, and it keeps sustaining and giving meaning to my life and the lives of countless others. Philosopher William Desmond points out how the myriad critiques of beauty pay "a secret tribute to the power of beauty" and the fact that beauty still moves us.[4] Similarly, as Annie Dillard observes, "Unless all ages and races of men have been deluded by the same mass hypnotist (who?), there seems to be such a thing as beauty, a grace wholly gratuitous."[5] Whether or not we are comfortable talking about beauty, it continues to stir up wonder, evoke desire, and form attachments.

Beauty is notoriously difficult to define, but I take beauty to be traces of divine glory in the natural world and human culture marked by an alluring wholeness of entangled forms, experiences, and ideas. Let me unpack that a little. I believe all beauty comes from God, since God created and sustains this world, and this God is indescribably beautiful as three-in-one, an alluring wholeness of entangled, trinitarian being. Some theologians are hesitant to call the triune God beautiful, preferring "glory" as the proper attribute,[6] but I have no qualms stating that God is Beauty just as God is Truth and God is Love. I also believe that beauty is a matter of wholeness and entanglement, which is to say beauty emerges when certain combinations, juxtapositions, and differences create a fitting, compelling whole. The traditional language for this is proportion, harmony, and perfection, but I think that language emphasizes wholeness more than the entanglement of differences, and both are a part of the allure of beauty.[7] For example, a forest is beautiful because it is a wholeness of entangled organisms, processes, histories, colors, smells, and sounds, all of which make a forest alluring, whether physically or experientially. Similarly, a piece of music is beautiful because of its alluring wholeness of entangled components, and so is a painting, a body, a conversation, a strategic plan, a prayer, a memory, or anything else. Objects can be beautiful, but so can experiences, actions, ideas, and the connections between all these. Furthermore, beauty cannot merely be reduced to what I like and find alluring, as beauty is a feature of divine being and created reality that I may not naturally appreciate in its fullness and variety because I lack attentiveness, receptivity, or imagination.

Rather than continuing to labor over the definition of beauty, however, this book focuses on the impact of beauty, which I believe is necessary for vibrant faith, hope, and love. Without beauty, our spiritual lives would wither and die, which is why *beauty is oxygen*. Sometimes beauty is like a slight breeze and other times it's like a gust, but it always carries with it the oxygen necessary for a breathable faith. If we are receptive, it can fill us with wonder, desire, and joy. To claim that beauty is oxygen is not to name it as an inanimate thing, some impersonal element on the periodic table. Rather, beauty is oxygen because through beauty we encounter the animating force of all life. Beauty is oxygen because it flows from the breath of God, the Creator Spirit.

Beauty is alluring—whether the beauty of artistry, the beauty of this wondrous and entangled world, or the beauty of human existence and interaction—because it witnesses to and participates in the beauty of God. If, as Dillard writes, "beauty and grace are performed whether or not we will or sense them," then "the least we can do is try to be there" and breathe them in like oxygen for our souls.[8]

What we make of beauty, of course, depends on what we make of anything within our framework of meaning. In this secular age, at least for those of us living in the West, it has become increasingly difficult to believe in anything outside of what philosopher Charles Taylor calls "the immanent frame," a disenchanted framework of meaning severed from the possibility of a transcendent, divine reality.[9] Within this framework, life is what we make it, and we don't need God or anything else to figure it out. Beauty may help us cope, but it's not connected to a deeper mystery. This book addresses that framework, the ache that often accompanies the inescapable search for meaning, and how beauty is an invitation into an enchanted, breathable life.

Faith traditions of all kinds have recognized the power of beauty, but in making the case that beauty is oxygen for our souls, I will be drawing primarily from my own Christian faith tradition while appreciating the wisdom of others. Even within the Christian tradition, there are numerous sub-traditions that deal with beauty in diverse and sometimes conflicting ways. The purpose of this book is not to outline all those theological and philosophical perspectives on beauty but to unpack the thesis that beauty is oxygen (chapter 1) and to develop a practical theology of beauty in relation to prominent dynamics of contemporary life: a buffered existence in which faith is increasingly difficult but desired (chapters 2–3), a battered existence in which hope can seem absurd yet vital (chapters 4–5), and a boring existence in which love is bland but still the longing of our hearts (chapters 6–7).

Although it's a good thing to be insulated from danger and harm, much of our contemporary life is also cut off from a sense of God's presence and action. How might beauty lead us to encounter God? Contemporary life is also full of traumatic forces, whether racial prejudice, gun violence, the ongoing effects of a global pandemic, or the climate crisis. How might beauty draw us forward in hope and motivate us to work for justice and the good of our neighbors? As contemporary life accelerates, so do boredom, isolation, and loneliness. Online entertainment and social media might provide a convenient escape, but they can also drive us further away from genuine encounters with beauty. How might true beauty give meaning and luster to our mundane lives?

Beauty is profusely available, whether in creation, culture, or human artistry. While beauty is profuse, it's not accurate to say that everything is beautiful. Traces of beauty are mixed with mangled and broken bits of reality. That's especially true within the shape of our human lives and all that we endeavor to make. To say, for example, that everything artistic is inherently beautiful depletes the idea of beauty into what philosopher Calvin Seerveld calls "an embarrassing catchall."[10] Many other thoughtful theologians have sounded a similar alarm. James K. A. Smith, for example, remarks that "there's so much more than beauty in this world."[11]

Could it be, however, that part of the problem is that our idea of beauty is not expansive enough? The poet Christian Wiman has written that "God goes belonging to every riven thing,"[12] and if God belongs to and identifies with torn things as well as pleasant things, then perhaps God's beauty goes belonging to all those things as well. If we embrace this idea, it will push our conception of beauty in several important directions.

First, it takes beauty beyond the subjective. God is the source of beauty, which means beauty involves but is not limited to our subjective perception and reception. We can recognize and receive beauty because it is given and revealed by God. There may be varying responses to beauty, but God's beauty "goes belonging" to this world whether we recognize it or not.

Second, it takes beauty beyond the static. God's beauty *goes*. It's on the move. Beauty appears and then hides; it arrives as a gift, over and over again. As such, beauty cannot be contained, controlled, or grasped and requires a posture of ongoing receptivity and attentiveness.

Third, it takes beauty beyond the abstract. God's beauty goes *belonging*. This beauty is not some ethereal, formless sublime, but a particular way the triune God goes belonging within the wholeness of our entangled lives.[13] Beauty is not a distraction from particulars. Rather, it draws us into the infinite drama unfolding in finite reality, what Wiman describes as "stone and tree and sky / man who sees and sings and wonders why."[14]

Finally, it takes beauty beyond the pleasant. God's beauty goes belonging *to every riven thing*. Beauty goes belonging to storms as well as sunsets. Beauty is there in dissonance as well as harmony. Perhaps it's easier to see how God's beauty goes belonging to riveted things, things that are all put together and tidy. But if Jesus, as the author of Hebrews confessed, is the "radiance of the glory of God and the exact imprint of his nature,"[15] and this Jesus was horrifically riven by crucifixion, then God's beauty goes belonging to wounds as well as empty tombs.[16] Beauty is oxygen by coming to us within the untidiness of life, and the entangled wholeness of beauty encompasses every riven thing.

Even if your framework of meaning differs from mine, I hope that what follows provides something refreshing, something hopeful, and a healthy dose of what G. K. Chesterton called "splendid confusion" that arises when encountering sacred mystery.[17] In keeping with this goal, what you'll find in this book is not a seamless argument but a series of provocations, a multi-threaded fabric of thought that weaves together my own experience of beauty with the encounters and reflections of others. Rather than continuous prose, you'll find snippets, fragments, and vignettes that build an impression and invite a slow, contemplative reading experience. Beauty often arrives in bursts and various forms, so I've written this book in a similar way, believing in the substance of style.

I would love for this book to be more than an intellectual exercise, to be formative as well as informative, and the best way to do that is to take your time, remember to breathe, and to utilize the "Questions and Practices" at the end either individually or in dialogue with others. Between sections, you'll notice an "O," the scientific symbol for oxygen. Each "O" is an invitation to take an actual breath: a deep, cleansing intake of oxygen. Take several. As you breathe, stay attuned to your body as well as your thoughts and feelings. Pause for a moment and attend to your surroundings, perhaps taking a sip of tea and noticing the beauty around you. As you do so, I hope you find yourself breathing a little more deeply of beauty.

CHAPTER I

Learning to Breathe

Roughly every three seconds, your brain autonomically signals the diaphragm and intercostal muscles to contract, making room for the spongy lungs to expand. As they swell, air rushes in through your nose and mouth, down the trachea, into the bronchi, and out to the tip of each tiny bronchiole, filling some 500 million alveoli. Oxygen in the air then diffuses from the capillary-encased alveoli into red blood cells, where it binds with hemoglobin and travels throughout your body, breaking down glucose into life-giving energy. Simultaneously, carbon dioxide diffuses from your blood into the alveoli and gets exhaled as muscles relax and compress the lungs. Without this process on rapid repeat, you would die in a matter of minutes.

"Let's see who can hold their breath the longest," my eight-year-old daughter challenges with gleeful moxy. She's been practicing under water. "Bring it on," I reply, confident that years of cross-country running and saxophone playing did my lungs some permanent good. We perform the countdown, the deep inhale, and the hold. . . . After twenty seconds, our bodies tense, and our faces turn red . . . just a few more seconds—mwahhhh! I barely beat her, and it fuels her competitiveness as well as her imagination. "Dad, is there oxygen in heaven where the angels live?"

> Wild air, world-mothering air,
> Nestling me everywhere,
> That each eyelash or hair
> Girdles; goes home betwixt
> The fleeciest, frailest-flixed
> Snowflake; that's fairly mixed
> With, riddles, and is rife
> In every least thing's life;
> —Gerard Manley Hopkins,
> "The Blessed Virgin Compared
> to the Air We Breathe"[1]

For humans with illusions of self-sufficiency, it is humbling to consider our utter dependence on the gift of oxygen. Food and water are also necessary to survival, but not with the same urgency and frequency. Oxygen occupies little of our conscious attention even while our bodies depend constantly on its intake. Life is indeed replete with "world-mothering" and body-sustaining air. Perhaps that's why it's so moving and more than a little mystifying to focus solely on your breathing. When you pay attention to your breathing, you are paying attention to your living body. You are paying attention to your life.

Everything needs it: bone, muscle, and even
While it calls the earth its home, the soul.
—Mary Oliver, "Oxygen"[2]

Try it for a minute.

Breathe in deeply through your nose, feeling your lungs fill completely with air.

Now slowly and gently breathe out through your nose, letting all the air escape.

Inhale deeply once again, staying present to the life-giving intake of oxygen.

Then exhale, savoring the expulsion of carbon dioxide.

Even though we can explain what's happening, it's still magical.

Deep, focused breathing provides many physical benefits: reducing anxiety, relieving pain, cleansing toxins, improving immunity, increasing energy, lowering blood pressure, improving digestion.[3] Take another deep, deliberate breath. No one's watching. And besides, it's free. Each time you see an "O" in between segments, consider it an opportunity to take a deep breath.

Deep, focused breathing also prompts life-giving questions. If breathing is usually involuntary, is it accurate to say that I am not in conscious control of my life and that life is, in fact, a gloriously repetitive gift? Is breath itself a prayer of thanks? What does it mean that the one thing I most need to survive is an invisible, tasteless, odorless gas? Where else do I see givens when I should see gifts? How else can my life be delightfully unself-centered?

Consider this: souls need beauty just like bodies need oxygen. Beauty diffuses into our souls like oxygen diffuses into our blood: freely, constantly, elementally. Beauty keeps our souls energized. Sound a little far-fetched? Perhaps it is, but near-fetched proposals aren't nearly as satisfying.

Soul is a splendid word with a checkered history. For one, the soul is not a pawn in a cosmic game of winning and losing. "Soul-winning" is a phrase I would love to ban from the Christian lexicon. I believe in conversation, but it's not a game. Also, the soul is not a substance that weighs twenty-one grams and drifts away when you breathe your last.[4] The soul is something more integrative, more holistic, more personal. More like something that breathes.

Translators render the Hebrew word *nephesh* as "soul," but in contrast to the plethora of English connotations, *nephesh* simply means "living, breathing being," a quality of animals as well as humans.[5] Creatures don't *have* a soul. They *are* a soul. When applied to humans, *nephesh* names not only who we are as breathing beings, but also our identity as beings consciously aware of breathing, people who think, feel, desire, perceive, commune with other souls, and seek the source of soul-life. We are breathing beings capable of soul-thirst, soul-praise, soul-satisfaction, soul-rest.

You, God, are my God,
earnestly I seek you;
I thirst for you,
my whole being (*nephesh*) longs for you.
—Psalm 63:1

Praise the Lord, my soul;
all my inmost being, praise his holy name.
—Psalm 103:1

If a man fathers a hundred children and lives many years, so that the days of his years are many, but his soul is not satisfied with life's good things, and he also has no burial, I say that a stillborn child is better off than he.
—Ecclesiastes 6:3[6]

Stand at the crossroads and look;
ask for the ancient paths,
ask where the good way is, and walk in it,
and you will find rest for your souls.
—Jeremiah 6:16

The Greek word for soul is *psychē*, again connoting a living, breathing being. More than just a breathing body, *psychē* is a body animated by life-breath. The English word *psyche* originates here, which in contemporary usage focuses on the mind and the origin of personality. Of the two English words *psyche* and *soul*, I'm drawn to *soul*, a word derived from Old English and carrying mystical overtones and intimations of cosmic drama. We may be individual psyches, but we are also souls caught up in a spiritual drama of soul-rest, soul-sorrow, soul-forfeiture, and soul-salvation.

"Take my yoke upon you and learn from me, for I am gentle and humble in heart, and you will find rest for your souls."
—Matthew 11:29

"My soul is overwhelmed with sorrow to the point of death. Stay here and keep watch with me."
—Matthew 26:38

"What good is it for someone to gain the whole world in exchange for their soul?"
—Mark 8:36

Even though you do not now see him now, you believe in him and are filled with an inexpressible and glorious joy, for you are receiving the end result of your faith, the salvation of your souls.

—1 Peter 1:8–9

Think of your soul like the lungs of your conscious, spiritual, perceptive, yearning being. Just as the body requires an external element to survive, our souls also depend on an external source of life. You might like to think of yourself as self-sufficient, self-reliant, and self-dependent. In reality, your soul is sustained by a constant flow of gifts, just like your body. Cut yourself off from the source, and your soul will suffocate.

In the Disney film *Soul*, Joe Gardner finds himself in the Great Before after dying and trying to escape from the Great Beyond (it's hard to explain; just watch the movie).[7] Joe is assigned to an unborn soul named 22 who is cynical about the fate of souls on earth. After Joe witnesses a piece of landscape fall on a group of souls who remain mysteriously unharmed, 22 explains: "Can't crush a soul here. That's what life on earth is for."

The soul-crushing dissolution of a marriage.
The soul-crushing doldrums of a day job.
The soul-crushing pain of disease.
The soul-crushing oppression of the vulnerable.

The soul-crushing loss of a child.
The soul-crushing violence of racism.
The soul-crushing isolation of individualism.
The soul-crushing futility of advancement.
The soul-crushing hatred of otherness.
The soul-crushing abuse of the weak.

The world is so beautiful in spite of the troubles.
—Terry Tempest Williams, *Erosion*[8]

Beauty is oxygen for a soul-crushing existence. Beauty blows through noxious environments, "nestling me everywhere."[9] If only we have eyes to see, ears to hear, noses to smell, tongues to taste, and hands to touch. Beauty permeates our souls through every sense. It shimmers through every crack, sounds through every silence, wafts down every street, lingers after every sip, radiates from every surface.

The soul-sustaining music of birdsong.
The soul-sustaining aroma of warm Spring rain.
The soul-sustaining bond between friends.
The soul-sustaining wonder of grace.
The soul-sustaining silliness of children.
The soul-sustaining horizon of the ocean.
The soul-sustaining joy of a wedding feast.

The soul-sustaining energy of a jazz quartet.
The soul-sustaining ache of belly laughter.
The soul-sustaining warmth of a winter fire.

⊘

He has made everything beautiful in its time.
—Ecclesiastes 3:11

⊘

Everything. It may be obvious how beauty is there in pretty sunsets and cute kittens, but beauty is also there in "every riven thing," because as Christian Wiman reminds us, "God goes belonging" there.[10] While some may contend that beauty is a luxury for the privileged, real beauty is accessible and necessary for every breathing being. Beauty is not merely in the eye of the beholder, because it originates from divine Beauty who beholds all. Poet Rita Dove claims that anyone who thinks beauty is only in the eye of beholder "has forgotten the music silk makes settling across a bared neck."[11]

⊘

Nothing else impresses itself upon our attention with at once so wonderful a power and so evocative an immediacy. Beauty is there, abroad in the order of things, given again and again in a way that defies description and denial with equal impertinence.
—David Bentley Hart,
The Beauty of the Infinite[12]

There are three things that are too amazing
          for me;
four that I do not understand:
the way of an eagle in the sky,
the way of a snake on a rock,
the way of a ship on the high seas,
and the way of a man with a young woman.
                                    —Proverbs 30:18–19

Beauty is there in a Van Gogh painting and in a flower in the sidewalk. Beauty is there in a Bach cantata and in a child singing her heart out, slightly off tune. Beauty is there in the poetry of the Psalms and in the misspelled note on my desk reminding me that "it's been a wile since we've ben on a dadi-dauter date so can you pleese skedule that?" Beauty is there in the vintage reserve saved for a special occasion and the "kombucha in a mid-century modern glass," which Ross Gay celebrates as a delight.[13] Beauty is there in ferocious storms and in flickering fireflies. As Gay observes: "how common a creature it seems before its cylindrical torso starts glowing, intermittently, at which point it is all of strangeness and beauty in one small body."[14] Beauty is there in straight and kinky hair, representational and abstract art, wrinkled faces and smooth ones, praise and lament. There is suitability in beauty, but there's also surprise.

We love to define things, but defining beauty can lessen the need for ongoing encounter and exploration. Bahar Orang puts it this way: "Beauty, like memory, can only be defined provisionally. There is no complete essay to write on beauty, no final word, no quintessential image. Please understand, beauty is not a problem to be solved; beauty is not a question to be answered; beauty denies enclosure and straightforwardness."[15] Ralph Waldo Emerson expresses a similar notion: "The beauty that shimmers in the yellow afternoons of October, who ever could clutch it?"[16]

In other words, beauty is not a thing that we can easily pin down, dissect, or fathom, which can be both a wonderful and challenging experience. In Dostoevsky's *The Brothers Karamazov*, Mitya wrestles with this in his confession to Alyosha: "Beauty is a terrible and awful thing! It is terrible because it has not been fathomed and never can be fathomed, for God sets us nothing but riddles."[17] Just because beauty is a riddle, however, does not mean it has to be terrible. Sometimes the best things in life are unsolvable. Certainly, the elusiveness of beauty can be frustrating and disagreements about what is beautiful can be confusing. But there is also something liberating about the mystery of beauty because it invites us to be humble and dependent. Beauty is not a thing to be grasped, possessed, or controlled; we receive it as a gift.

Receiving beauty as oxygen requires dismantling the idea that beauty has no practical function, that it exists purely for leisurely contemplation rather than soul survival. Even in nature, beauty is useful. The vibrant red plumage of a northern cardinal is useful for attracting a mate and claiming territory. The unique patterns and tints on each Cuban snail, influenced by diet, prevent predators from solidifying a search image for their next meal. Beauty attracts and detracts and is necessary for the survival of a species. What about the survival of souls? The survival of faith, hope, and love? The survival of wonder and worship? And not just survival, but the possibility of a human being fully alive? Perhaps theologian Wendy Farley is right when she writes: "Without food, our bodies die. Without beauty, our spirits die."[18]

The human soul needs actual beauty even more than bread.

—D. H. Lawrence,
"Nottingham and the Mining Country"[19]

An upright piano occupied a prominent place in my home growing up. My parents insisted that all four children take piano lessons, and as the youngest, the pattern was deeply ingrained by the time I took the bench. Our home was filled with piano music—some delightful and some rather plunky—every single day of my life, until all my siblings left for college. I'm deeply grateful for this habit now, despite feeling aggravated by the daily practice mandate then. There are scores of studies showing the benefit of learning a musical instrument for brain development, and I'm sure my parents had that in mind as they checked on the completion of my charts. But under and through all the discipline, I believe there was a deeper impulse than ensuring my intellectual growth. Even though it remained largely unstated, I sensed a deep desire for beauty to permeate our home and lives by filling it with song and melody. It's a desire I share and experience watching my own kids practice piano, knowing that beauty sometimes sounds like Mozart and other times like "Mary Had a Little Lamb."

Brian Doyle claims we were made for beauty like fish are made for water:

> You have poetry slots
> Where your gills used to be, when you lived
> inside your mother.
> If you hold a poem right you can go back there.
> Find the handle.
> Take a skitter of words and speak gently to
> them, and you'll see.[20]

And—if I may add to Doyle's image—you have music slots, dance slots, theatre slots, and film slots, not to mention thunderstorm slots, flower slots, star slots, and as many other slots as there are forms of beauty. I like to imagine the gills are still there, filtering out oxygen from the constant flow of beauty.

It is difficult
to get the news from poems
yet men die miserably every day
for lack
of what is found there.
—William Carlos Williams,
"Asphodel, That Greeny Flower"[21]

At the same time, beauty is far more than useful or necessary. The beauty of creation is over the top, leaving scientists scratching their heads.[22] Is it necessary for a peacock's tail feathers to be so enormous and intricate? While some measure of beauty is useful for attracting mates and repelling competitors, the extravagance defies easy explanation. Likewise, the beauty of human artistry has many uses in everyday life, but it also "needs no justification."[23] The beautiful high priestly garments created for tabernacle worship in the wilderness were useful for setting the priests apart as covenant representatives and mediators, but what's the purpose of sewing blue, purple, and scarlet pomegranates around the hem of the robe?[24] There might be some symbolic meaning, but mostly it just makes them more beautiful. Art doesn't need to instruct, evangelize, or symbolize to be valuable. In other words, beauty has many uses, but it also transcends utility. Paradoxically, beauty is both necessary and gratuitous.

> To claim beauty as gratuitous is not to refuse a purpose
> or use to beauty; it is simply to claim that beauty exceeds
> any particular purpose or use to which a person puts it.
> —Natalie Carnes, *Beauty*[25]

I remember reading that there are around 400,000 identified species of beetles in the world, comprising about 25 percent of total identified species on earth. I had to google that and fact check it multiple times. Seriously? Why, for heaven's sake, does the world have so many beetles, and why such variety and intricate forms? While no doubt there are a myriad of evolutionary answers to this question, none of these reasons quite explain, it seems to me, the sheer extravagance (and volume) of beetles. Why is there a beetle shaped like a violin (*Mormolyce phyllodes*)? Or the Hercules beetle (*Dynastes hercules*) that can carry 850 times its weight? Or jewel beetles (*Buprestidae* family) prized for beetlewing jewelry and decorations around the world? Or why the common ladybug (yep, also a beetle: *Coccinellidae*) that flits its red, polka-dotted body around the garden eating aphids and looking sharp? In addition to scientific reasons, I'm compelled by a theological and aesthetic reason: God is displaying a profuse variety of beauty in all these beetles.

I love how Dietrich von Hildebrand, while tackling dense, philosophical questions about beauty in his two-volume *Aesthetics*, can't resist celebrating the excessive variety of beauty in the natural world.

23

What beauty fruits have, for example, an apple, an orange, a cherry, a plum! What beauty of form there is in an ear of corn, or indeed in a root! What a wealth of forms comes into play even in the pits of fruit! How perfectly everything is formed, even down to the smallest structures! And what of trees—an oak, a beech, a poplar, a plane tree, and above all a cypress, a pine tree, an olive-tree, an evergreen oak; an orange tree with ripe fruits, an apple or cherry tree in bloom! What a world of beauty in each individual type! What nobility of form, of color, of the shape of a trunk, the crown, and the leaves![26]

Beauty is oxygen, not only because it's necessary, but because it's a gift from God. Priest and chef Robert Farrar Capon wrote a toast that I love to share at communal feasts:

> To a radically, perpetually unnecessary world; to the restoration of astonishment to the heart and mystery to the mind; to wine, because it is a gift we never expected; to mushroom and artichoke, for they are incredible legacies; to improbable acids and high alcohols, since we would hardly have thought of them ourselves; and to all being, because it is superfluous. . . . We are free: nothing is needful, everything is for joy. Let the bookkeepers struggle with their balance sheets; it is the tippler who sees the untipped Hand. God is eccentric; He has loves, not reasons. Salute![27]

God's beauty is so powerful that too much of it can be dangerous. As critical as oxygen is for our physical lives, any diver will
tell you about the danger of excessive oxygen. It's called oxygen
poisoning. Can beauty poison in a similar way? Moses wanted
to see the glory of God, a full presentation of God's beauty, to
assure him that God would indeed fulfill his promises. God
let Moses see a glimpse of his beauty, but only his back. Why?
Because the full brunt of God's beauty would kill him.[28] If we
take in too much beauty too quickly, not taking the time to
process and enjoy it, we can suffer from a form of beauty poisoning. It's that feeling of exhaustion when you rush through
an art museum and try to take it all in. It's the "fear and trem-
bling" that emerges when you realize that God's beauty is not
only external but also internal, propelling you forward in the
journey of being saved.[29]

While our souls need beauty like our bodies need oxygen, it
is wise to proceed with caution. God's beauty, after all, is not
always what we might expect. In *The Lion, the Witch and the
Wardrobe*, when Susan discovers that Aslan is a lion and not
a man, she asks, "Is he—quite safe? I shall feel rather nervous
about meeting a lion." To which Mr. Beaver promptly responds,
"Safe? . . . Who said anything about safe? 'Course he isn't safe.
But he's good."[30] Beauty isn't safe. But it's good and true.

Beauty is oxygen for people who struggle to find meaning beyond the self, coming like a fresh breeze into the suffocating atmosphere of "me, myself, and I." To encounter beauty of any kind, whether in creation or the arts, is an opportunity to experience a radical unselfing. While encounters with beauty can have deep emotional impact, beauty is far more than therapeutic. It moves us beyond self-centeredness, liberates us from illusions of control, and brings us into transformative encounters with a transcendent God who draws near within our material world.

Beauty is oxygen for people who struggle to find and maintain hope. True beauty is not sentimental, carrying along with it the wounds of our existence, as we see in the person of Christ. In a time of racialized violence, environmental crisis, and growing inequalities, the beauty of the arts and creation can bear witness to a weighty, anchored hope, one that does not evade the reality of evil and injustice. Beauty can awaken us to see things as they currently are while also giving glimpses of how things could and will be. These visions activate our individual imaginations and collective will for costly action within situations of oppression, suffering, trauma, and injustice.

Beauty is oxygen for people who struggle with boredom and find little to love with abandon. Beauty allows us to breathe deeply within ordinary times and spaces. Rather than moving from one meaningless day and season to another, we can be filled with wonder when we are alert to the beauty of creation and the glory of ordinary things. As Hopkins writes, there is "the dearest freshness deep down things" despite the fact that "all is seared with trade; bleared, smeared with toil."[31] In addition, by participating in the beauty of worship, we learn and embrace our role in the drama of God within the mundane, where the story of each day is caught up in the cosmic drama of loss and renewal.

CHAPTER 2

A Suffocating Life

O nce upon a time, most people experienced life in a porous way.[1] Spiritual forces swirled through the atmosphere, flowing freely in and out of permeable beings. Just as air contains both beneficial and hazardous gases, so the spiritual forces of good and evil mixed and mingled and made people vulnerable to harm as much as health. For porous souls, the world was an enchanted, wondrous, wild, and dangerous place.

Once upon a time, as in there really was a time when people believed that good and evil spirits interacted with their soul.[2] Spiritual disciplines, sanctioned liturgies, and sacred pilgrimages allowed souls to inhale as much divine oxygen as possible while exhaling the demonic like carbon dioxide. Like physical breathing, the flow of oxygen into the soul was constant, critical, and largely involuntary.

A Suffocating Life

Once upon a time, as in, "Isn't this just a fairytale?" Greenhouse gases may be killing our planet and harming our lungs, but our souls—if such a thing even exists—are now largely cut off from God and spiritual forces in everyday life. We have sealed off the old portals through which enchanted air used to flow, confident that the soul can circulate its own recycled air. We are now free to fly through life without worrying about how our souls will breathe. We can move about the cabin of our secure inner world, tapping into entertainment to provide the thrills once linked with enchanted existence.[3] We are safe and secure and doing just fine, thank you very much.

"I'm fine" has become a convenient smokescreen for our aching souls. We might say we're fine, but like Ross in *Friends*, it comes out all "loud and squeaky,"[4] because we often feel the opposite.[5] Philosopher Charles Taylor calls this the "malaise of immanence," which is deeper than an aversion to your best friend hooking up with your sister (*à la* Ross's forced "fine"). It's an overarching loss of meaning, an increasingly hopeless search for significance, a painful sense of emptiness.[6] In other words, the "malaise of immanence" is the sneaking suspicion that despite feeling safe and fine, we are slowly suffocating. It's a growing dissatisfaction with recycled air, a feeling of claustrophobia as we travel through life in the pressurized cabin of the self. It's a sense of bland repetition that we seek to augment with personal entertainment, personal possessions, and personal style. Do you relate? Don't forget to breathe.

Like a big house in an expensive neighborhood, our inner lives are expansive but protected. They have curb appeal but are not open for visitors. And just like a big house in an expensive neighborhood, the walls and high hedges are there to keep intruders with evil intentions out. . . . But we didn't see that eventually we would secure this inner world so extensively that we could keep even God out. Once this happened in modernity, there became a tangible sense, like in neighborhoods with expensive houses, that to achieve this safety you must lose the excitement of connection and engagement, making you safe but bored.

—Andrew Root, *The Pastor in a Secular Age*[7]

Buffered from demons along with the divine.
Buffered from risk along with reward.
Buffered from danger along with excitement.
Buffered from external authority along with external meaning.
Buffered from disasters along with delights.
Buffered from offensive ugliness along with compelling beauty.
The malaise seeps in.
How long will the oxygen last?

Homer: Kids, how would you like to go to Blockoland?
Bart and Lisa: Meh.

Homer: But the TV gave me the impression that—
Bart: We said, Meh.
Lisa: M-E-H. Meh.[8]

Meh is a fitting way to express the malaise of buffered souls. At the end of 2009, BBC News asked its readers to send in words that they thought most defined the first decade of the twenty-first century. *Meh* reached the top twenty, along with *i-*, *truthiness*, and *Facebooking*, all common lingo of a buffered existence.[9] Popularized by *The Simpsons* TV show, *meh* verbalizes the malaise experienced in almost every area of life, including spirituality. For roughly three years, *The New York Times* published "The Meh List" in their "One-Page Magazine," a weekly list of things that are "not hot, not not, just meh." Everything was game for "The Meh List," even The Meh List itself, which was the final entry of the final list, right after "muffins" and "never going to bed angry."[10]

The growing sense of *meh* about life is connected to the condition of being buffered from any reality, divine or otherwise, that could provide overarching meaning or purpose. Charles Taylor calls this the "immanent frame"[11] in which the primary point of reference is the individual self rather than a transcendent or supernatural reality. As a result, individuals are responsible to forge an authentic way through life and construct some meaning out of it. When all that effort and discipline gets exhausting or ceases to be attractive, however, what you're left with is *meh*.

One way to deal with the *meh* malaise is to celebrate the self-made life G-Eazy style. The American rapper, with the melodic assistance of Bebe Rexha, created an anthem for buffered souls with the song "Me, Myself, and I."[12] He celebrates life as a "solo ride until I die" without the need to depend on anyone or anything. At the same time, he admits that music gives his life meaning and is keeping him alive. Even G-Eazy recognizes that beauty is oxygen, but he struggles to make sense of it.

The declaration of G-Eazy's soul-independence ("I don't need a hand to hold") alongside the reality of beauty-dependence ("the music fills me good") creates what Charles Taylor calls "cross pressure."[13] Cross pressure is the ache for significance on the solo ride, the desire for magic when all seems mechanistic, the need for meaning beyond myself even when it seems like myself is all I have. Cross pressure is feeling *meh* but wanting to experience *wow!*

I don't believe in God, but I miss him.
　　　—Julian Barnes, *Nothing to Be Frightened Of*[14]

William Desmond wonders, Why is there such a thing as "soul music" but not "self music"?[15] His answer is robust and philosophically nuanced, but here's a simple summary: *soul* names a porous identity with an openness to the mystery of being, whereas *self* names the buffered identity of me, myself, and I. Souls can lose themselves in music, whereas selves sing only for themselves, even if they might long for more.

A Suffocating Life

Few movies portray cross pressure—experiencing malaise but longing for wonder—better than the 1999 film *American Beauty*.[16] It seems like the Burnham family has everything a middle-class American family would want, but everybody feels meh. In a search for meaning within the malaise, Lester quits his corporate job, buys his dream car, and fuels his obsession with a high-school cheerleader. In the meantime, his wife Carolyn has an affair and their daughter Jane pursues a relationship with Ricky, their obsessive, weed-dealing neighbor. Anything is permissible, and chaos ensues.

Beauty, especially in its sexualized form, becomes a thing to consume in a futile attempt to ease the ache. Ricky, the one person who seems attentive to beauty, is ridiculed as mentally ill, especially when he claims to see beauty in a dead bird, a frozen homeless woman, or a floating plastic bag. In sharing his footage of the plastic bag with Jane, Ricky searches haltingly for words to describe the experience: "It was one of those days when it's a minute away from snowing. And there's this electricity in the air, you can almost hear it. . . . And this bag was just . . . dancing with me, like a little kid begging me to play with it. . . . It helps me remember, I need to remember . . . sometimes there's so much beauty in the world. I feel like I can't take it, and my heart is going to cave in."

Even Lester feels the cross pressure as he reflects on his tragic life: "It's hard to stay mad when there's so much beauty in the world. Sometimes I feel like I'm seeing it all at once, and it's too much. My heart fills up like a balloon that's about to burst." Both Ricky and Lester experience beauty as oxygen, but it takes them to the brink of annihilation. Their hearts can't take in genuine beauty without facing their incapacity.

If the buffered soul was merely a cultural condition, then there might be a self-help solution, but the problem is deeper than that. Theologically speaking, being born into this fallen world means inheriting a curse and an assumption that we can work our way out of it.[17] Martin Luther described this curse as the self-centered curvature of human nature. This is our fallen nature, and it "not only turns the finest gifts of God in upon itself . . . but it also seems to be ignorant of this very fact."[18] What Luther means is that despite our best efforts to get beyond ourselves, to love God and others and the world, we find it impossible to escape the gravity of self-interest. To make matters worse, we live under the illusion that we can. We think we can be the hero of our own private story, but in reality we need another hero to redeem us from the curse.[19]

One cover for the ninetieth anniversary edition of *The New Yorker* shows a male figure curved over his phone with a butterfly fluttering unnoticed above his head.[20] This is a fitting portrayal of the buffered soul. The physical curvature of our spines as we hunch over personal electronic devices demonstrates— and aggravates—the inward curvature of our souls. The essential problem is not the technology, since personal devices can provide opportunities to share and receive beauty. The problem is our buffered condition, our curved nature, our natural spiritual posture. Just as physical postures hunched over devices limit our capacity for physical breathing, so hunched spiritual postures limit our capacity for our souls to breathe.[21]

We can be sure that whoever sneers at her [beauty's] name
as if she were the ornament of a bourgeois past . . . can no
longer pray and soon will be no longer able to love.
—Hans Urs von Balthasar,
The Glory of the Lord[22]

Beauty in all its forms has the potential to liberate us into a more
expansive, porous, breathable life, but if Luther is right, there
is only so much beauty we can receive without a fundamental
unselfing, a radical reorientation, a whole new nature. We need
a new heart so that our old heart won't cave in or burst, like the
characters in *American Beauty*.[23] We need new lungs capable
of breathing in the fullness of beauty, which includes eternal
beauty. The meh we feel is a sign of our sickness unto death,
but diagnosing the sickness is the first step toward healing.[24]

The ancient city of Laodicea (in modern-day Turkey) had a water
problem. Hot springs in nearby Hierapolis had a healing, medic-
inal effect. Water in nearby Colossae was cold and refreshing. But
Laodicea didn't have access to hot or cold water. Anything drink-
able had to be piped in, and by the time it arrived the water was
tepid and potentially contaminated. Like the air in their souls, it
was not hot, not cold, just meh, and it was making them sick.

To the angel of the church in Laodicea write: "These are the words of the Amen, the faithful and true witness, the ruler of God's creation. I know your deeds, that you are neither cold nor hot. I wish you were either one or the other! So, because you are lukewarm—neither hot nor cold—I am about to spit you out of my mouth. You say, 'I am rich; I have acquired wealth and do not need a thing.' But you do not realize that you are wretched, pitiful, poor, blind and naked."

—Revelation 3:14–17

The buffered soul says: I've got it made; I don't need anything from anyone. I'm good with the independence of me, myself, and I. I have financial independence because of my wealth. I have political and social independence because of my power. I have spiritual independence because of my wisdom. But underneath the bravado, the malaise and cross pressure builds to a boiling point.

According to pastor-theologian Sam Wells, breaking free from our buffered state requires realizing that everything we are and have is a gift. "All the things we thought were ours—our achievements, rights, possessions, entitlements, fallbacks, supports— were never really ours after all. Our breath was not ours, but was made up of air we didn't make that came from outside us, and was breathed by lungs we didn't construct, enfleshed by food we didn't direct, processed by a stomach we couldn't control."[25]

Listen then to the Messenger: you don't realize that your buffered soul is suffocating. You need to open humble hands and receive wealth you could never earn. You need to open healed eyes and see beauty you could never imagine. You need to get dressed, get up, and open the door into a whole new world. Open it, and beauty will rush in so you can breathe again.[26]

Some may think that repentance is a matter of feeling sorry for doing bad things and begging God for forgiveness. But that's a buffered way to understand repentance. True repentance is recognizing you're not the center of the story. It's not about you; it's about the beauty of God. Repentance is a matter of acknowledging your buffered condition and calling on the Spirit to blow through your life.

Repent of entitlement and receive everything as a gift.
Repent of your declaration of independence and accept
    your dependence.
Repent of soul suffocation and embrace a breathable life.
Repent of meh and open your life to wonder.
Repent of malaise and believe in a deeper magic.
Repent of deadened heart and ask for openness and availabil
    ity to beauty.
Repent and let the Spirit relieve the cross pressure.

Repent, believe, and breathe in the beauty of the world and
the beauty of God.

Dear God, I cannot love Thee the way I want to. You are
the slim crescent of a moon that I see and my self is the
earth's shadow that keeps me from seeing all the moon.
The crescent is very beautiful and perhaps that is all one
like I am should or could see; but what I am afraid of,
dear God, is that my self shadow will grow so large that
it blocks the whole moon, and that I will judge myself
by the shadow that is nothing.

—Flannery O'Connor, *A Prayer Journal*[27]

Seeing even a sliver of beauty is a reminder that there is always
more waiting to be discovered, like the dark side of the moon.[28]
Each encounter is an invitation beyond the cramped quarters
of the buffered soul into a space where we are free to feel the
breeze of beauty and to breathe again.

CHAPTER 3

The Breeze of Beauty

The moment we entered the doors of the Orthodox church, we started breathing more deeply. Our friends had invited us to join them for The Service of the Graveside Lamentations on the Friday evening before Orthodox Easter, which also happened to be the eve of our long-awaited sabbatical from church ministry. We were tired and longing for beauty. Making our way to the balcony, we sat in silence and gazed at magnificent murals depicting the saints and story of God. Several icons seemed to glow, fire-lit by the setting sun, and for the next three hours we immersed ourselves in the drama of Christ's burial through the beauty of word, song, candlelight, incense, movement, and silence. Slowly the drama of our little world diminished and the world of a loving Father, dying Son, and sustaining Spirit loomed large in our imaginations. The priest led us to acknowledge and name the energy of the Evil One, but it was no match for the Breath of God, the Breath that animated lifeless dust into breathing souls, the Breath that filled the lungs of a three-day-dead Christ, the

Breath that filled our souls in this worshipful encounter with traces of divine glory.

> One thing I ask from the Lord,
>   this only do I seek:
> that I may dwell in the house of the Lord
>   all the days of my life,
> to gaze on the beauty of the Lord
>   and to seek him in his temple.
>
> —Psalm 27:4

Midway through our sabbatical we hiked in the Children's Eternal Rainforest in Costa Rica and decided to practice an extended time of forest bathing, *shinrin-yoku* as it's known in Japan. Winding through a tentacular maze of towering trunks and sprawling roots, we attempted to take in the vast forest life with every sense. The beauty was overwhelming, so it helped to receive it in small doses: gazing upward at the crown of this enormous tree, touching the bark of that gnarly one, pausing to listen to this howler monkey, noticing the bright flash of that strawberry poison dart frog, smelling the sulfuric steam near this thermal vent, cautiously and respectfully avoiding the coiled body of a fer-de-lance. Beauty belongs to particular places and creatures and is a feature of their interrelatedness and entanglement as well as their wholeness.

> To bathe in a forest is to be immersed in a grace that
> permeates the world, to feel an immanent power and
> beauty that is everywhere, whispering.
>
> —M. Amos Clifford,
> *Your Guide to Forest Bathing*[1]

❀

What if the whisper of immanent beauty is the same divine
Breath that hovered over the primordial waters?[2] What if that
whisper of beauty is so compelling because it's a breeze that
blows from a transcendent source? What if the forest provides
oxygen for our souls just as much as physical oxygen for our
bodies? It's no surprise that John of Patmos envisioned the
leaves on the tree of life healing the nations.[3]

❀

What do places of worship and forests have in common? For
one, they are both places where God's beauty goes belonging.
Both contain traces of divine glory. Both are environments
where you can breathe deeply, filling lungs and soul in equal
measure. Both poke holes in a buffered existence, allowing a
transcendent breeze to filter in. Of course, temples and forests
are not unique in these ways. We could say similar things about
a Wes Anderson film, a rocky beach on Lake Superior, an Aretha
Franklin album, a South Carolina swamp, a Romare Bearden
painting, a wildflower-flecked alpine meadow, or a Wendell
Berry poem. If you're open to it, beauty will stir up something
within you beyond a bland *meh*. As singer-songwriter Beck
conveys: "It's like wow! It's like right now. Oh wow!"[4]

Wow can mean a lot of things. There's the self-promoting "wow, I'm awesome" as expressed by Post Malone who "made another hit 'cause I got bored" and just to make people say "wow."[5] Then there's the snarky, sarcastic "wow, you're incredible" as conveyed by Kate Bush in her Pink Floyd–inspired commentary on acting on stage and in life.[6] Or there's the seductive "wow, you're amazing" as celebrated by Zara Larsson.[7] These *wows* merely bounce around the echo chamber of a buffered life, barely able to alleviate the meh. Is there a lament lodged within these shallow *wows*? A longing for the song to be more than mere entertainment? A desire for truly authentic performances? A craving for intimacy to mean something more mysterious? A longing to breathe?

One of my oldest daughter's first words was *wow*. A monarch butterfly floating through the front yard: *wow!* The thunder rumbling and rolling on a hot July afternoon: *wow!* A vanilla cupcake with one flickering candle: *wow!* As we grow, *wow!* often gives way to *why?* and *what for?* and *whatever.* We get self-conscious and self-occupied, but beauty continues to draw us out. If we cease to say *wow*, the rocks will cry out for us.[8]

> Listen hard now to how we all say goodbye
> and maybe and wait-just-a-minute,
> not hearing the world say back to us wow.
> —Bill Manhire, "Wow"[9]

The *wows* elicited by genuine encounters with beauty are deeper and more resonant than the shallow *wows* of a self-centered life. In encountering beauty, there is an unbuffering, an unselfing, a decentering, a beckoning to something beyond, transcendent, and soul refreshing. Elaine Scarry, professor of aesthetics at Harvard, puts it this way: "At the moment we encounter something beautiful, we undergo a radical decentering. . . . It is not that we cease to stand at the center of the world, for we never stood there. It is that we cease to stand even at the center of our own world. We willingly cede our ground to the thing that stands before us."[10]

Have you ever gotten lost in a lover's eyes?

Have you ever been carried away by a piece of music?

Have you ever had your breath taken away by the color of the sky?

Have you ever been engrossed in a powerful story?

Have you ever been captivated by "the underwater operas of whales" and "the prayer rituals of bees"?[11]

Have you ever been "flabbergasted by the endurance of love and delight" in the presence of a baby?[12]

How does it feel to cede your ground to beauty?

Did you know that being decentered could be delightful and reveal a whole new world?

The late poet-philosopher John O'Donohue observed: "To behold beauty dignifies your life; it heals you and calls you out beyond the smallness of your own self-limitation to experience new horizons. To experience beauty is to have your life enlarged."[13] Wendy Farley, professor of spirituality at Rice University, agrees: "beauty is more than a respite for a worn-out or self-indulgent soul. It is our recognition that something exists other than the projections and passion of our ego minds." In short, beauty offers "liberation from the prison of egoism."[14]

I love walking, and it's not just about the exercise. While walking does lower stress, strengthen immunity, build muscles, and provide many other health benefits, walking for me is also a way of moving about in the world where God's beauty goes belonging. If I'm preoccupied, walking in our neighborhood redirects my attention away from my own swirling thoughts to songbirds, cloud formations, neighbors sitting on porches and walking their dogs, front yards strewn with children's bikes and toys, and a world swirling with beauty that has nothing to do with me. Walking is good for my ego.[15]

What good does it do, C. S. Lewis asks, to read good literature? What is the draw? Quite simply: "we seek an enlargement of our being. We want to be more than ourselves." We want to see the world with other eyes, hear the world with other ears, experience the world in different bodies. "Here, as in worship, in love, in moral action, and in knowing, I transcend myself; and am never more myself than when I do."[16]

What if being unselfed is the way to become our true selves? What if we need to be decentered to find the true center? What if we must lose our lives to save them? What if decreasing is the way to increase? What if it's possible to find a breathable faith?

The danger is to seek beauty merely for personal consumption rather than allowing ourselves to be overcome and consumed by beauty. Pleasure and enjoyment are not bad, but what if true enjoyment is found by immersing and losing oneself in the allure of beauty rather than merely focusing on personal happiness? Philosopher Dietrich von Hildebrand describes the fitting disposition for encountering beauty as "the reverent humble surrender of self . . . being truly moved and profoundly gladdened in such a way that one forgets oneself and does not seek one's own pleasure." By contrast, "the aesthete aims at skimming off the cream, so to say. He is never really moved or overcome."[17]

Within a buffered existence, aesthetic experience is often an escape or distraction. But within a porous existence, beauty invites us into what Frederick Buechner calls "something richer, realer, more immediate, and more shimmering, even if it's only the moment of the frog jumping into the pond."[18] Beauty is what stops us in our tracks and calls us to pay attention. This is, Buechner explains, what good art does. It says, "Stop thinking. Stop expecting. Stop living in the past. Stop living in the future. Stop doing anything and just pay attention to *this* . . . allow yourself to be seized by this."[19]

You have seen many things, but you pay
no attention;
your ears are open, but you do not listen.

—Isaiah 42:20

If we desire to receive beauty as oxygen, we need to cultivate attentiveness to what Matthew Crawford calls "the world beyond your head."[20] We need to be disposed outward. We need a disponibility—a state of availability—to beauty on earth as it is in heaven. Disponibility or availability is the precondition for being dazzled and transformed by beauty.[21]

A simple breath prayer can be effective for cultivating availability and attentiveness to beauty, even in the most mundane moments.

Inhale: Open my soul and senses.
Exhale: To all the beauty here.

Dietrich von Hildebrand writes about the kind of soul-receptivity needed to receive beauty: "To what extent does someone open his soul when he sees a beautiful landscape? To what extent is he willing and able to receive this beauty? One who is preoccupied with other things, such as cares or plans, may indeed perceive that the landscape is beautiful, but he will not be capable of enjoying it and letting himself be affected by it." Readiness to receive beauty requires "being free, being opened, the absence of everything that disturbs, being completely receptive in the moment."[22]

Could it be that when we pay attention to beauty we are opening ourselves to God? Writing on the history of Christian spirituality, Rowan Williams observes: "To be absorbed in the sheer otherness of any created order or beauty is to open the door to God, because it involves that basic displacement of the dominating ego without which there can be no spiritual growth."[23]

When I consider your heavens,
the work of your fingers,
the moon and the stars,
which you have set in place,
what is mankind that you are mindful of them,
human beings that you care for them?

—Psalm 8:3–4

47

Encountering and considering the beauty of the stars opens the possibility that God both created the stars *and* cares for us. While this experience of beauty does not *prove* God is the transcendent Creator of the beautiful, starlit sky, it at least opens the door of imaginative *possibility*. This is what Charles Taylor is talking about when he commends "enlarg[ing] our palette of points of contact with fullness."[24] Stargazing is a point of contact with fullness. Jesus encourages us to consider the lilies because they are a point of contact with fullness.[25] So are the impressionistic water lilies of Monet and other forms of artistry. These encounters with beauty can liberate us from "the prison of egotism" and open the door to a God who crafts and sustains beauty and who cares for buffered little me. Not everyone who breathes in the beauty of the stars or the lilies will acknowledge that beauty comes from God, but taking time for wonder is at least a step closer toward acknowledging that all this beauty might be God's breath.[26]

If the stars should appear one night in a thousand years, how would men believe and adore; and preserve for many generations the remembrance of the city of God which had been shown! But every night come out these envoys of beauty, and light the universe with their admonishing smile.

—Ralph Waldo Emerson,
Nature and Selected Essays[27]

The Webb telescope recently revealed more wonders: distant colliding galaxies, gas-giant exoplanets, dying star systems. The internet exploded with images. People who rarely share more than filtered selfies were suddenly sharing unedited photos of the universe. The world, as many news articles observed, was collectively *wowed*. The explanations, however, were mixed. Some quoted Psalm 8 and described these photos as displays of God's glory. Others quoted scientific studies on the age of the universe and celebrated these images as further indication that God has little if anything to do with such beauty. Nevertheless, these breathtaking glimpses of the universe stirred awe. People on all sides explained their experience as a kind of unselfing, an acknowledgement that we are not the center of the universe. Much of the online conversations exist, however, in what Charles Taylor calls "a kind of middle space, neither explicitly believing, but not atheistic either, a kind of undefined spirituality."[28] This is the essence of "cross pressure," sensing that beauty carries spiritual significance but not having an adequate framework to explain it.[29] At the same time, Taylor observes, "many people are not satisfied with a momentary sense of wow! They want to take it further, and they're looking for ways of doing so."[30]

Agreement within the social media flurry: beauty dislodges us from the center of the story. Disagreement within the social media flurry: does beauty unself us into relationship with God? Agreement within the social media flurry: beauty has a transcendent quality. Disagreement within the social media flurry: does transcendent beauty have a name?[31]

Talk of transcendence in nature and the arts is widespread, but it's not often precise. As a result, musician and theologian Jeremy Begbie thinks transcendence in the arts needs to be "redeemed" from its anthropocentric, vague, generalized, and formless expressions.[32] If the arts have the power to unself us from "the fantasy that we are in control" and dispossess us from "the inward pull of the domineering human ego," then what role does the triune God play in that unselfing process?[33] How does the nature of the triune God as both transcendent (i.e., beyond the world) and immanent (i.e., within the world) help us understand and receive beauty?

Imagine that for all eternity God has been sharing and giving beauty in a dance of relation between Father, Son, and Spirit and that creation is a wondrous extension of this beauty. If that's true, then created beauty is an expression of God's desire to be lovingly entangled with creation and no chasm exists between God's transcendent beauty beyond the world and the immanent beauty within the world. God is transcendently beautiful as revealed through the beauty we can experience in this world, through immanent entanglement with creation, not despite it. God's beauty remains wholly other while totally belonging to all God has made. Although not writing from within a Christian imaginary, Bahar Orang is more accurate than many theologians by observing how "beauty is nothing if not an essential detail of relation, of entanglement."[34] The core Christian mystery is that the immanent beauty of God that shines "through all and in all" is the transcendent beauty of God that exists "over all."[35]

Commenting on the theology of Gregory of Nyssa, Natalie Carnes puts it this way: "The best statement of God's radical transcendence is God's utter immanence to all things, and God's utter immanence is possible because God is radically transcendent." In other words, God can belong to this world without ceasing to be God precisely because God is beyond the world. Similarly, God's beauty is revealed within the particulars of the world because God's beauty is beyond the world. "Beauty ... [points] to God's beyond-ness while celebrating the particulars of God's nearness."[36]

It is one thing to acknowledge how God's transcendent beauty is encountered within a beautiful world. It is quite another thing for buffered people to receive this beauty as oxygen for their souls. Even if God's invisible beauty can be clearly seen, it's possible to remain unmoved, inattentive, and stuck in self-centeredness.[37] What makes one person respond to a starry night with a worship-inducing *wow!* and another to respond with an apathetic *meh*? What's the difference between someone who merely escapes into John Coltrane's music and someone who is led by his music out of self-centeredness and into the beautiful and supreme love of God? Just because we have eyes doesn't mean we see beauty for what it is. Even though we have ears, we may not hear the call of beauty.[38] We need a new openness and availability to beauty, a transformation of our senses, "a *returning* that we are unable to initiate ourselves."[39]

0

Here's how the old story goes, told from the perspective of God's Beauty, which is one with God's Truth and Goodness.

In the beginning was Beauty, and Beauty was
    with God, and Beauty was God.
Through Beauty all things were breathed
    into being.
In Beauty was oxygen for all.[40]
Infinite Beauty was revealed in galaxies, blood
    vessels, and trees.
With one special breath, Beauty gave life to
    human beings-in-beauty.[41]
Beauty began to swirl and play in ten
    thousand places.[42]
Despite all this, humanity rejected their depen-
    dence on Beauty.
They wanted a beauty they could control
    and consume,
a beauty they could enjoy on their own terms,
a beauty that they could use to make a name
    for themselves.
They channeled the beauty of the earth
    into production,
the beauty of artistry into idols,
and the beauty of humans into objects.
But Beauty cannot be oxygen as a product,
    idol, or object.
Beauty can only be oxygen as presence, sacra-
    ment, and gift.

Beauty is not a thing to be used, purchased,
    or achieved.
Beauty must be encountered, witnessed,
    and received.
The invitation, then, is to belong to Beauty
just as Beauty belongs to the world.
The invitation is to breathe in and be
    with Beauty
just as Beauty became flesh to breathe and be
    with us.[43]
To do so, however, requires new breath within
    these dry bones,[44]
a new heart and new lungs for taking in Beauty
    as oxygen.[45]
It requires Beauty to breathe on us in a
    new way.[46]

According to theologian Karl Barth, God's triunity is the "secret of God's beauty," since the mutual relations and self-giving love of Father, Son, and Spirit generate God's radiance, splendor, and joy.[47] God's beauty is the glorious, mutual entanglement of Father, Son, and Spirit who belongs to and gets lovingly entangled in covenantal relationships with creation and a chosen people, despite their ongoing resistance and rejection. This peaceful and persistent entangling led to God's violent mangling through crucifixion. There is vulnerability and death at the heart of divine beauty. God's beauty led him to the cross, and it beckons us to take up our cross daily and die to self.

"All beauty arises out of vulnerability,"[48] writes luthier Martin Schleske, because beauty emerges within the entanglements of real relationships in which we experience both pain and pleasure. We will discover the beauty of the earth when we are entangled with it rather than floating above it. We will perceive the beauty of other creatures when we relate to them in personal and responsible ways.[49] We will encounter the beauty of others when we stay entangled in communal life. We will be transformed by the beauty of God when we are entangled with Christ, much like branches are entangled with the vine.[50] To be porous and entangled is to be vulnerable yet available to the breeze of beauty.

Buffered souls have a hard time imagining how vulnerability and entanglement are pivotal for encountering beauty, but the arts can enliven our imaginations and keep us attentive to beautiful entanglements with others. Makoto Fujimura argues that "the arts provide a perfect vehicle to move past clogged, cluttered self-absorption into the reliable communal body to experience the Spirit's leading."[51]

The beauty of the arts can foster an empathetic imagination and justice-loving entanglements with others.[52] Narrative arts—novels, plays, and some films—are particularly effective at enabling us to enter imaginatively into the concrete situations of others and to motivate moral and pastoral engagement more powerfully than journalism or historical reportage.[53] The beauty of Alan Paton's novel *Cry, the Beloved Country* opened my middle-school eyes and heart to the horrors of racism and structural injustice more than purely historical accounts of South African apartheid.[54] The beauty of Garrison Keillor's novel *Lake Wobegon Days* helped me appreciate and see God's presence within the quirky characters and everyday dramas in my own Minnesotan small-town reality and subsequent places of residence and ministry.[55] The beauty of Terrence Malick's film *The Thin Red Line* stirred my empathy with those who have experienced the trauma of war and fostered within me a passion for nonviolence.[56] The beauty of Jonathan Larson's musical *Rent*, and its subsequent film adaptation, expanded my compassion and respect for artists and their unique struggles and gifts.[57] Beauty is oxygen for just and generous neighboring.

Other forms of art also have this capacity to help us love our neighbors and therefore contain what Alan Noble calls a "disruptive witness."[58] I recently spent an afternoon in Charlotte's Mint Museum and was drawn to the vibrant color and larger-than-life scale of Kehinde Wiley's *Philip the Fair*.[59] Moving closer, I reveled in the detail of the floral patterns and facial expression, contemplating the juxtapositions and layers of meaning. Wiley's painting is based on a stained-glass work depicting France's King Philip IV, a treacherous yet arguably handsome historical figure ironically named "Philip the Fair." Standing in the same pose as King Philip IV, the African American male in Wiley's painting wears jeans and an Astros jersey. The placard reads: "Wiley bestows the power and authority of Eurocentric Western painting onto his anonymous models who emphasize black masculinity and strength. The floral patterning of the background highlights the figure and subsequently offers Wiley's subject a place of prominence and gives expression to men who often occupy a place of invisibility in society."

The painting drew me out of myself as I entered its narrative. Physically, I was drawn close instead of remaining at a distance. Intellectually, the painting presented truth in a fresh, allusive way for me, getting behind some of my natural defenses and biases and coaxing meaningful interaction between new ideas. Emotionally, I felt both sorrow and anger as I considered the lives all too often rendered invisible by greedy leaders, powerful institutions, and unjust systems. Volitionally, the painting forced me to evaluate how my own actions and habits, particularly as a leader, are never neutral and either enhance or degrade the glory of my neighbors.

Our lives only begin, our moral struggle only commences, once we've loved something enough to want to leave ourselves behind. That can be painful—but ideally it's never worse than bittersweet.
          —Timothy G. Patitsas, *The Ethics of Beauty*[60]

Beauty moves the imagination and creates a desire to love. The opposite is also true. "Hate," observes the whisky priest in Graham Greene's *The Power and the Glory*, "[is] just a failure of imagination."[61] The best art invites us to "imagine our neighbors as ourselves" and can therefore widen the circumference of our love.[62]

While God's beauty within creation and human artistry has unselfing power, we should not assume that this decentering, empathetic movement happens automatically, nor should we place our hope in the innate qualities of any created or artistic object. Given our curved nature and the gravitational pull of self-interest, being unbent by beauty is an act of God's grace.[63] After all, it is *God's* transcendent beauty that permeates the world, and therefore whatever liberation from self-centeredness we might experience by encountering beauty is pure gift and the overflow of divine love. Jeremy Begbie writes: "true unselving . . . takes places as we are caught up in a costly and transforming movement of God in and through us: in other words, as we share by the Spirit in the self-dispossession of the Son and Father."[64]

Enjoyment of artistic beauty is a wonderful thing, but it pales in comparison to entanglement with transcendent, trinitarian beauty. C. S. Lewis issues a fitting word of caution: "The books or music in which we thought beauty was located will betray us if we trust to them; it was not *in* them, it only came *through* them and what came through them was longing."[65] What we really want, Lewis comments later, is to be entangled with beauty. "We don't want merely to *see* beauty. . . . We want . . . to be united with the beauty we see, to pass into it, to receive it into ourselves, to bathe in it, to become part of it."[66]

If Christ is the revelation of God's beauty, then replacing "Christ" with "beauty" in Saint Patrick's Breastplate prayer is a striking way to consider the ways in which God's beauty is oxygen for our souls.[67]

> Beauty with me,
> Beauty before me,
> Beauty behind me,
> Beauty in me,
> Beauty beneath me,
> Beauty above me,
> Beauty on my right,
> Beauty on my left,
> Beauty when I lie down,
> Beauty when I sit down,
> Beauty when I arise,
> Beauty in the heart of all who think of me,
> Beauty in the mind of all who speak of me,
> Beauty in the eye of all who see me,
> Beauty in the ear of all who hear me.

CHAPTER 4

Asphyxiations of Counterfeit Beauty

My son loves to draw volcanoes, and he takes the process seriously, usually gifting me the finished product so I can post it proudly by my desk and contemplate lava's terrible beauty. One recent afternoon, however, things turned out differently. Somewhere in the middle of the process, with crayons in multiple shades of red and orange clasped in his hand, he groaned in frustration and pushed the half-completed volcano drawing aside. "What's wrong?" I asked from the kitchen. "It's ugly," he moaned. I walked over and glanced at the drawing, which was remarkably like previous versions, and tried to be encouraging. Hoping to avoid a meltdown, I said: "It looks beautiful to me." With a look of disgust at my apparent lack of artistic discernment, he violently crumpled the paper and threw it to the floor. "I hate it."

We tend to hate and destroy things we think are ugly, but who gets to say what's ugly or beautiful? What if our perception of what is ugly or beautiful is skewed? What if something that's ugly to you is beautiful to me? Who decides what gets preserved and what gets destroyed, what's worth loving and what's worth hating? What is ugliness anyway?

There's a dangerous connection between perceived ugliness and destruction. If you want permission to destroy something, you just need to be convinced that it's ugly, or at least uglier than the alternative. Behind most acts of destruction and preservation is a powerful aesthetic, a clear delineation of what is ugly and what is beautiful. An aesthetic vision drives ethics by guiding what we view as desirable, worthwhile, and excellent.[1] Our vision of what is beautiful and ugly, in other words, propels our commitment to either preserve or destroy, appreciate or ignore, love or oppress, serve or dominate.

Among many other things, racism is a distorted aesthetic that associates beauty (and therefore goodness and truth) with a particular skin color. Not only that, but within European colonial history, this racial aesthetic was fused with what Willie James Jennings calls a diseased Christian imagination.[2] Within this aesthetic, racialized beauty became a tool of evaluation, hierarchy, and oppression. Perceiving nonwhite people as ugly (as well as uncivilized and irreligious) was justification for their enslavement and destruction.

This racial aesthetic, deeply embedded within European and North American art, links dark-skinned people and dark landscapes with barbarism and backwardness while associating light-skinned people and light landscapes with purity, progress, and holiness. You see it in Daniele da Volterra's sixteenth-century painting of David's battle with Goliath (1550–1555), where David is white-skinned and blond, and Goliath is swarthy and raven-haired. You see it in John Gast's portrayal of *American Progress* (1872), where white-skinned Angel Columbia leads the charge into a dark land full of beasts, wildness, and native people, leaving in her wake a light land full of white people, domesticated animals, and orderly development. You see it in Warner Sallman's famous *Head of Christ* (1940) with his flawless Caucasian skin and flowing auburn hair. If this is the standard form of beauty, it should be resolutely rejected. It's toxic.

In Sally Rooney's novel *Beautiful World, Where Are You?*, a character named Eileen suggests a theory that "human beings lost the instinct for beauty in 1976, when plastic became the most widespread material in existence."[3] She proposed this theory not only because plastic itself is a colorless, ugly substance, but also because of how plastic was incorporated into a culture of disposability that has accelerated environmental degradation. One could posit other points in history when human beings lost their instinct for beauty. What about 1933, when the Third Reich established the first concentration camps for people they deemed ugly and unfit for society? Or perhaps 1830, when American President Andrew Jackson signed the Indian Removal Act and began forcing the First Nations off their beautiful ancestral lands? Or 1619, when the first African

slaves arrived in colonial Virginia? Or 1418, when Portugal began their first colonial voyage to Africa? Or 1095, when Pope
Urban II launched the first crusade against Muslim-controlled
Jerusalem? In these examples, violence and injustice were in-
trinsically related to the failure to see beauty and worth in
all people as well as a failure to see the beauty of the world
as something to be carefully stewarded rather than conquered
and harnessed. If you want, you could trace the loss of an instinct for beauty and its ethical implications all the way back
to when Adam and Eve exchanged true beauty for a tasty bite
of self-centered knowledge.

In 2014, Eric Garner pleaded "I can't breathe" eleven times before
he died in a police chokehold on the New York City streets. Six
years later, on the streets of Minneapolis, George Floyd gasped
the same last words. As a recent article highlighted, "I can't
breathe" were the last words of at least seventy others who died
in law enforcement custody during the 2010s: "The majority of
them had been stopped or held over nonviolent infractions, 911
calls about suspicious behavior, or concerns about their mental
health. More than half were black."[4] Beauty can't bring these
people back to life, but can beauty help others breathe, especially
those who live in fear? If beauty is going to be oxygen in an age of
"I Can't Breathe," it cannot be the twisted aesthetic of so-called
colonial beauty, racist beauty, or the beauty of a white Jesus.
These counterfeit forms of beauty asphyxiate.

According to one report, global spending on skin whitening was an estimated $8 billion in 2020 and increasing.[5] Why? Because in many cultures lighter skin is perceived as lovelier, and with loveliness comes less discrimination and greater opportunity for vocational and social advancement. Not only does skin whitening reveal and perpetuate a diseased racial aesthetic, but it also uses toxic ingredients such as steroids, hydroquinone, and mercury. Countries across Africa have rightfully banned skin-whitening products, but that has often spawned an extortionary underground market. Despite a growing movement celebrating darker skin tones, colorism is proving a tenacious legacy.[6]

Beauty is not white. Nor is beauty Western or American. There are beautiful things about America, but to sing unreservedly "America the Beautiful" is deeply problematic when her history includes "pilgrim's feet, whose stern, impassioned stress a thoroughfare for freedom beat across the wilderness,"[7] often beating down Native land and life along the way. Freedom for a select few is not beautiful. Similarly, there are beautiful white people, but whiteness is not the beauty standard. Racism involves an oppressive, grotesque way of seeing the world that ignores the beauty inherent in particular places and people for the purpose of possessing them.[8] Beauty is most evident within the entanglement of differences and moves us to desire and preserve those differences. Beauty lies in what Willie James Jennings calls "boundary-transgressing" kinships and communions that take us beyond bland homogeneity.[9]

My family and I are currently part of a church community comprised of a diverse array of cultures, skin tones, economic backgrounds, and languages. Each member is beautiful in their own right, but the combinations and juxtapositions within the community are even more striking when we gather together. It makes me think about the revelation of John when he sees "a great multitude that no one could count, from every nation, tribe, people and language."[10] All their robes are washed white, but their bodies are every glorious color.

Diversity, mixture, entanglement, and difference are beautiful because they witness to the unified diversity of a God who is both one and three.[11] A pure blue sky is beautiful, but it's even more beautiful when blended with yellows, pinks, and purples. A solid black night sky is beautiful, but even more so when scattered with billions of sparkling stars. Just as monotheism is not the whole story of a triune God, monochromatic schemes don't capture the whole story of beauty. Beauty emerges within a profusion of difference, in touching, mingling, mixing, and in what David Bentley Hart calls "diverging and converging lines, developments, and transitions."[12]

All things counter, original, spare, strange;
Whatever is fickle, freckled (who
knows how?)

With swift, slow; sweet, sour;
adazzle, dim;
He fathers-forth whose beauty is past change:
Praise him.
—Gerard Manley Hopkins, "Pied Beauty"[13]

But how do we praise God in a world full of trauma? Doesn't this emphasis on beauty distract us from seeing reality in its raw brokenness? According to writer Ta-Nehisi Coates, good art enlightens and brings us face to face with reality as it is rather than providing specious hope.[14] In his book *Between the World and Me*, Coates pleads with his son never to look away from the reality of white supremacy over black bodies, a visceral experience that "dislodges brains, blocks airways, rips muscles, extracts organs, cracks bones, breaks teeth." Beauty can be summoned as an excuse to look away. The "widely shared picture of an eleven-year-old black boy tearfully hugging a white police officer" may be beautiful in a certain sense, but not if it's a feel-good distraction from reality.[15] A deep aesthetic can expose our emotions and potentially reshape them. A shallow *aesthetic*, which Coates rightly warns us against, merely acts as a comfortable *anesthetic*. Real beauty should be oxygen, not sleeping gas.

If Beauty Incarnate experienced blocked airways and cracked bones in his crucifixion, how does that challenge our typical ways of conceiving beauty? Is this what C. S. Lewis meant when he coined the term "Terreauty"?[16] How does this form of terrible beauty equip us to see God's beauty belonging to every riven thing, including sacrifice? Rather than distracting us from the reality of war and trauma, what if beauty can endure suffering and begin to heal our battered souls?

Makoto Fujimura writes about the unique conception of beauty embedded in the Japanese word for beauty, two ideograms meaning "sacrificial sheep" and "great." Here we see the "overlap of . . . decay with permanence, death with life . . . beauty and sacrifice."[17] Sometimes beauty is hidden. Sometimes beauty is silent. Sometimes beauty emerges through great sacrifice. Beauty, Fujimura confesses, "is indeed terrifying."[18]

Sentimentality deprives beauty of its power. According to Jeremy Begbie, sentimentality trivializes evil, placates emotions, and avoids costly action.[19] An easy target for oversentimentalized art is the painting of late American artist Thomas Kinkade. Widely known as the "painter of light," Kinkade claimed to be a Christian, and his stated purpose was to bring light into people's lives, making them feel good. Whatever his actual motives, making people feel good is a brilliant business plan. Kinkade once attributed the success of his paintings to "portray a world without the Fall," a world without evil, a world with nothing to elicit anxiety.[20] The world of Kinkade paintings, of course, is not the world in which we live. It's not the world experienced viscerally by Coates and his son, and it's not the world experienced by Kinkade himself, who died at the age of fifty-four from acute intoxication. Kinkade's art fails to put us in touch with "a terrible beauty" and does not give us a vision for how trauma can be transformed. It just tries to soothe.

All such sincere, Sunday Schoolish artificial projects are pseudo-Christian and their innocuous presentations not only devastate understanding art but also misrepresent and take the bite and grit and life out of the Christian commitment.

—Calvin Seerveld,
A Christian Critique of Art and Literature[21]

I keep thinking about how genuine beauty has bite and grit, something that hits you in the gut instead of always eliciting pleasant feelings. I think of the magnificent beauty of God that the psalmist says shines forth with fire and tempest.[22] I think of the entangled beauty of nature that depends on an endless cycle of life, death, and rebirth. I think of the intimate beauty of a relationship that navigates through the choppy, nauseating waters of conflict only to arrive on the other side somehow more whole and vibrant. I think of the mysterious and terrifying beauty of a black hole. I think of the uncontrollable beauty of my children that makes my heart ache because I know their hearts will break. I think of the sacrificial beauty of a God who chose to be broken for us and enter the abyss.

Mary Oliver wrote: "The beauty and strangeness of the world may fill the eyes with its cordial refreshment. Equally it may offer the heart a dish of terror. On one side is radiance; on another is the abyss."[23] God's beauty is even stranger, with the radiance of a resurrected Christ emerging from the dark abyss of death. It may seem like a contradiction, but our experience of beauty can include what Christian Wiman calls a "bright abyss."[24]

In 2013, American singer Pharrell Williams released his song "Happy" from the soundtrack for *Despicable Me 2*. It soared to the top of the charts, and the music video has been viewed more than a billion times on YouTube. In 2014, Pharrell followed up with a twenty-four-hour video of people of all shapes, sizes, and ages dancing and singing to "Happy" in different locations around the clock. The video is infectious, and the more you watch it, the more you begin to believe that "happiness is the truth" and "can't nothing bring me down." Is this sentimentalism gone wild or joyful resistance in the face of trauma? More recently, an online conversation surged when a Twitter user expressed his annoyance at the song and Williams retweeted with one word: "same." The floodgates opened and more people began admitting their annoyance and dislike of "Happy." Why? Because, as the listeners shared, it's emotionally simplistic, sonically boring, and lyrically naïve. It's classic sentimentality. It may make you feel good for a while, but it doesn't stick, like a sugar rush. Can you experience happiness without first experiencing grief? Can you appreciate the light without the darkness? Is there joy without suffering? Happiness is not the truth, but beauty is.

> God's beauty embraces death as well as life, fear as well as joy, what we might call the ugly as well as what we might call the beautiful. It reveals itself and wills to be known on the road from the one to the other, in the turning from the self-humiliation of God for the benefit of man to the exaltation of man by God and to God.
> —Karl Barth, *Church Dogmatics*[25]

While death itself is not beautiful, in Christ death becomes a place that mediates the beauty of God. While fear and ugliness are not beautiful, in Christ they mediate a kind of beauty that experiences and overcomes them. If that is true, then we cannot seek beauty only in things that make us happy. If we know God's beauty on the road from self-humiliation to exaltation, then we need to discern beauty in shadows as well as landscapes of light. Sometimes beauty eases our sorrows and sometimes it makes us feel them more intensely. Beauty is a kind of perfection, but as theologian Steven Guthrie writes, it is "a perfection that can accommodate scars."[26]

Sorrow is so woven through us, so much a part of our souls, or at least any understanding of our souls that we are able to attain, that every experience is dyed with its color. This is why, even in moments of joy, part of that joy is the seams of ore that are our sorrow. They burn darkly and beautifully in the midst of joy, and they make joy the complete experience that it is. But they still burn.

—Christian Wiman, *My Bright Abyss*[27]

If anything challenges a sentimental or overly simplistic view of beauty, it's the fact that Jesus, the revelation of God in human flesh, was not outwardly attractive. As the prophet Isaiah tells us: "He had no beauty or majesty to attract us to him, nothing in his appearance that we should desire him."[28] Beauty elicits desire, but there was nothing desirable about his appearance. Beauty draws our gaze, but we hid our faces from him. We are invited to see a different kind of beauty in the one who carried our sorrows and healed our wounds.[29] If God is beauty, and God is fully revealed in Jesus, then this should influence the kind of beauty we expect to encounter, the kind of beauty that can be oxygen for our souls.

If Jesus is the ultimate revelation of beauty, do we also need the beauty of art and nature for our souls to breathe? Isn't the most important thing in the face of injustice more justice rather than more beauty? In a time of climate crisis, isn't beauty a distraction from the real work of preservation? If someone needs shelter, what good is the beauty of a rainstorm? Beauty may seem like a detour from mercy, healing, and justice, but there are many ways in which beauty motivates, enhances, and sustains this work. Critic Jason Farago asks: "Why listen to music, why look at art, why go to the theatre when war is raging?" His answer, in short, is that the arts "enable us to discern, in the daily tide of images and insanities, any meaning at all." Faced with "an undammable river of content" and constantly scrolling images, good art can make us stop long enough to consider the meaning of what is being destroyed and what might remain.[30]

◌

Another well-known objection to extravagant beauty is voiced by Jesus's disciples:

> While Jesus was in Bethany in the home of Simon the Leper, a woman came to him with an alabaster jar of very expensive perfume, which she poured on his head as he was reclining at the table. When the disciples saw this, they were indignant. "Why this waste?" they asked. "This perfume could have been sold at a high price and the money given to the poor."[31]

Where the disciples see waste, Jesus sees beauty. "Why are you bothering this woman? She has done a beautiful thing to me."[32] Jesus answers his own question. The disciples were bothering this woman because they failed to see any function for beauty beyond its ability to fix a problem like poverty. This woman's act of pouring expensive perfume on Jesus's head is beautiful, however, because it is an extravagant sacrifice anticipating and anointing the extravagance of Jesus's imminent sacrifice on the cross. Witnessing such extravagant beauty therefore should not diminish the disciples' capacity to serve the poor. Rather, it should empower them toward costly action.

Something similar happens when we encounter the extravagant beauty of creation. While I might for a moment be distracted by the beauty of a yellow swallowtail butterfly, my next reaction is a desire to care for it. While a rainforest can be a place of solace and self-forgetfulness, it also stirs in me a passion for preservation. While I can lose all sense of time snorkeling among fish and their underwater world, it also gives me a renewed sense of urgency in a world of warming oceans. While the profusion of wildflowers in a forgotten ditch may seem random and unnecessary, it's that randomness, wildness, and extravagance that I'm moved to protect. Even while natural beauty elicits enjoyment for its own sake, our encounter with natural beauty also propels us to honor, preserve, and cultivate more of it. In an age of climate emergency and anxiety, therefore, we need more opportunities to appreciate beauty, not less. Beauty is never a waste.

Every September, vibrant red spider lilies erupt in our backyard. After pushing their long stems up from the ground, they explode in a display of delicate petals and stamen. Their beauty is extravagant. Some of them, however, despite digging up their bulbs and moving them to flower beds, keep popping up in the middle of our mowed lawn. Every year, therefore, I'm faced with a conundrum: let the spider lilies grow or mow the lawn? Do I let the weeds grow along with the flowers or do I cut everything down in pursuit of order and the American ideal of the manicured yard? Those wily spider lilies serve as an annual reminder that beauty is first and foremost not mine to cultivate and control; it's a gift to receive. While there is a time and place for orderly cultivation, it's also crucial to keep the edges wild and to rejoice that this world is beautiful with or without our well-intentioned stewardship. This is a good reminder, especially in an age of ubiquitous human impact on nature.[33] Beauty is not a human invention; it's not ultimately about us.

A sober look at our world shows that the degree of human intervention, often in the service of business interests and consumerism, is actually making our earth less rich and beautiful, ever more limited and grey, even as technological advances and consumer goods continue to abound limitlessly. We seem to think that we can substitute an irreplaceable and irretrievable beauty with something which we have created ourselves.

—Pope Francis, *Laudato Si'*[34]

It's true that we humans can make a mess of beauty, but we also have an opportunity to shine light both on the abuse of beauty and the persistence of beauty in the world. Sara Schumacher explains how artists can play the roles of servant, apprentice, and prophet amid our environmental crisis. They can help us wake up and "inhabit the horror" of environmental destruction (consider Aronofsky's film *Mother!*) and keep us attentive to beauty and its invitation toward kinship with creation (think of the BBC documentary *Planet Earth*). Schumacher contends, "The loss of our ability to see beauty means we do not see creation for what it is and do not treat it in the way it deserves.... Thus, it is important that artists, when they create, do not overlook the beauty that still remains in the world."[35]

There is so much beauty in the world, but it's not always what we think. If beauty is to function as oxygen for battered souls, it needs to be released from the prison of a racial aesthetic, expanded beyond the boundaries of a sentimentalized aesthetic, and freed from the constraints of a dominating, anthropocentric aesthetic. We need to learn to encounter beauty in the faces of diverse kin, in places of both shadow and light, and in experiences of what philosopher-poet Bayo Akomolafe calls "these wilds beyond our fences."[36]

In her poem "How to Prepare for the Second Coming," Abigail Carroll incites us to commit a sort of theft:

> with deft lock-picking and shrewd hand, steal
> back the hours you fed to the hungry god
> of work,

then squander them on hydrangeas,
        Wordsworth,
voluntary sidewalk repair.[37]

Work can be beautiful, but if we desire beauty to be oxygen, we may have to get used to "squandering" our time. Eventually, what at the beginning felt like squandering may begin to feel like worship.

CHAPTER 5

Healing Breaths of Fresh Beauty

S oon after the death of George Floyd in Minneapolis, seventeen artists in Charlotte, North Carolina, like artists in many cities around the world, collaborated to create a massive street mural witnessing to the truth that *Black lives matter*. Each artist took a different letter of that mantra, fashioning it on the uptown asphalt in their own unique style and together making a beautiful, collective expression of lament and hope. Even before the mural began, however, a debate surfaced among community leaders about whether these murals were enhancing or distracting from the movement for racial justice. Was this an example of fiddling while Rome burns? Was this mural merely a performative distraction from the necessity of policy changes on a political level and heart changes on a personal level? Or might the artistry and creativity of this mural impact politics and move hearts in its own unique way? There is frivolous fiddling, to be sure, but there's another kind of fiddling that reminds us that after Rome burns, a new city can rise from the ruins.

How can we justify art and beauty when the world is in shambles? The world, of course, has always been in shambles, at least since the Eden rebellion. This is nothing new. I suppose then we should rephrase the question: how can we justify art and beauty at any time and place given the inevitable brokenness of things and the persistence of injustice? In his essay "Learning in Wartime," C. S. Lewis raises the stakes to an eternal level by asking "how it is right, or even psychologically possible, for creatures who are every moment advancing either to heaven or to hell, to spend any fraction of the little time allowed them in this world on such comparative trivialities as literature or art."[1] The crisis of human society lies in the shadow of an infinitely larger crisis, says Lewis, so we can't delay the search for beauty on the assumption that life will someday become more secure.

We should seek and create beauty *all* the time, even (especially!) during times of war because on one level, "it is our nature."[2] Ignoring beauty is dehumanizing and will intensify the crisis. By contrast, it is healthy and humanizing to nurture beauty in a time of crisis. Failing or refusing to remain open to beauty when circumstances are dire will only exacerbate an already stifling environment, while being receptive to beauty creates avenues for healing and hope. It can taste like a surprising feast in the midst of scarcity (consider Isak Dinesen's story *Babette's Feast*).[3] It can sound like singing on the frontlines (consider Christian Carion's film *Joyeux Noël*).[4] It can look like adding color to drab, painful places (consider Enrique Chiu's *Mural de la Hermandad* on the US-Mexico border).[5] It can feel like simply enjoying your surroundings while waiting in line or at a stoplight rather than scrolling through your crisis-driven newsfeed. Amidst all the chaos, beauty humanizes and brings meaning.

The good news according to Ecclesiastes: life is hard and life is a vapor, but it's still beautiful, so breathe in as much beauty as you can. Work is toilsome, so enjoy the beauty of the daily grind. Your body will get sick and die, so delight in the beauty of food and drink. Oppression is rampant, so embrace the beauty of friendship. Your libido will fade, so revel in the beauty of sex. All is meaningless under the sun, so soak in whatever traces of glory you can capture. Here's how Eugene Peterson paraphrases the beauty-centric commands in Ecclesiastes 9:7–10:

> Seize life! Eat bread with gusto,
> Drink wine with a robust heart.
> Oh yes—God takes pleasure in *your* pleasure!
> Dress festively every morning.
> Don't skimp on colors and scarves.
> Relish life with the spouse you love
> Each and every day of your precarious life.
> Each day is God's gift. It's all you get
> in exchange
> For the hard work of staying alive.
> Make the most of each one!
> Whatever turns up, grab it and do it.
> And heartily!
> This is your last and only chance at it,
> For there's neither work to do nor thoughts
> to think

In the company of the dead, where you're most
certainly headed.[6]

November 2016 began an excruciatingly difficult and tragic season for our church, our family, and for me as a pastor. At the
beginning of the month, a dear friend in her twenties, a church
member and campus minister at a local university, died suddenly from a blood clot, leaving behind a husband debilitated
by grief. In the middle of the month, the teenage son of prominent church leaders took his life, leaving behind him a turbulent
wake of unanswerable questions and angry lament. At the end
of the month, the mother of a church staff member died from
health complications having lived a long—but not nearly long
enough—life. We were battered by grief and then battered some
more. During all this loss and pain, our son Chalmer was born.
He was pure gift; he was the way God's beauty came to us in im-
penetrable darkness. I remember arriving home one evening—
exhausted, shattered, speechless—taking my newborn son in
my arms, and weeping. And then laughing. Then crying some
more, partly from sadness, partly from joy. I remember feeling
twinges of guilt along with the grief: How can I possibly find
so much pleasure in this wriggling life when surrounded by so
much death? Why do I get to smell the sweet fragrance of my
son's head when another father has lost his? This too is meaningless. Yet this too is how beauty works: arriving when we need it
the most, arriving when we least expect it, arriving to remind us
that this life is precious and precarious and worth relishing.

I read John Piper's *Desiring God: Meditations of a Christian Hedonist* toward the end of high school and was absolutely enthralled. The idea that I can glorify God *by* enjoying him forever transformed my view of Christian obedience and discipleship, and I became an eager evangelist for "Christian hedonism." Later in my journey, however, I started feeling dissonance with various aspects of Piper's framework, not least of which his portrayal of husband-led marriage as the ideal matrix for desiring God. In looking at the book recently, what struck me was the lack of engagement with Ecclesiastes (he only quotes 3:11 in passing), especially since Ecclesiastes is Scripture's hedonistic manifesto. It seems this is related to Piper's concern that worldly beauty easily (inevitably?) distracts us from divine beauty: "The tragedy of the world is that the echo [read: worldly beauty] is mistaken for the Original Shout [read: divine beauty]. When our back is to the breathtaking beauty of God, we cast a shadow on the earth and fall in love with it. But it does not satisfy."[7] While I agree there is danger in turning our backs on the beauty of God, I also believe that God's beauty belongs to this world in astonishing ways. While we can ignore God's relationship to the world and thus idolize creation, we can also disregard that relationship in a way that makes worldly beauty constantly and notoriously suspect. Perhaps this is why Piper includes a chapter about prayer but not one about prairies, a chapter about Scripture but not one about other captivating stories, a chapter on evangelistic missions but nothing on the mission of gardening, woodworking, wine-making, or festive living. If we ignore the beauty of God, we'll get lost in the beauty of the world. But if we ignore the beauty of the world, we might miss God, and our souls will suffer.

If beauty is oxygen, we might have to stop skimping on colors and scarves.[8] The Preacher of Ecclesiastes would cheer us on. The healing path for battered souls involves *both* reveling in ephemeral beauty *and* remembering an eternal Creator.[9] The key is to keep them connected: we can remember our Creator *by* reveling in ephemeral beauty.

In his *Confessions*, Augustine admits that in his younger years he was obsessed with lovely things but didn't recognize them as the presence of a beautiful God: "You were with me, and I was not with you." Eventually, the reality of divine beauty broke through, reorienting his life.[10] In reading Augustine, however, one wonders if after his conversion he ever recovered the ability to enjoy the beauty of "various arts and crafts in clothing, shoes, vessels, and manufactures of this nature, pictures, images of various kinds, and things which go far beyond necessary and moderate requirements and pious symbols."[11] If the beauty of these things comes from "that beauty which is higher than souls," then the problem lies not in the beauty of this artistry but in the failure to be attuned to how it's an expression of God's beauty. If that's true, then to "entangle my steps in beautiful externals," as Augustine laments, is not necessarily a temptation, but a way of staying entangled with a beautiful God.[12]

Art and beauty give pleasure and delight, which is a balm for battered souls. But they also give expression to pain. Art matters in a world gone awry because it enables us to articulate and share incalculable grief, trauma, abuse, and loss. Out of the bentness of suffering we get the bent notes of the blues. Out of a sense of God forsakenness we get the poetic laments of the Psalms. Out of a traumatic childhood and tortured spirituality we get Edvard Munch's painting *The Scream*.[13] Out of the growing meaninglessness of modernity we get Samuel Beckett's play *Waiting for Godot*.[14] Out of the experience of money not wiping away tears we get Kendrick Lamar's song "United in Grief."[15] When the pain and burden is too deep for words, art can "tell all the truth but tell it slant," as Emily Dickinson reminds us in her poem.[16] Expressing the pain can begin the process of healing. Sharing the burden can lift it enough to take a deeper breath.

Jeremy Begbie comments on the power of artistic beauty—music in this case—not only to express our feelings but to reshape them:

> Music can voice not only what we do feel but what we could or perhaps should feel. Is this not what Bob Dylan did for a whole generation in the 1960s? Is this not what "We Shall Overcome" did for thousands in the civil rights struggle? It changed those who sang it; it helped them find fresh hope and courage. And is this not what the greatest hymns and songs do? They not only help us sing what we already experience emotionally: to some extent they also educate and re-form our emotional experience.[17]

Why do we need beauty most of all when battered and traumatized? The answer is as complex as the trauma, which is essentially the ugly story (or stories) we believe, inhabit, and embody because of painful, horrific experiences. In other words, trauma is not merely something bad that happened in the past, but the ugliness and pain that permeates one's body and life in the present.[18] As image-bearers of God, we are beauty-breathing beings, but trauma narrows those airways as well as the attachments through which we experience beauty. Timothy Patitsas explains it this way: "In trauma we find our lives organized around an experience of ugliness, the opposite of the Beauty given to us in our relationship with God."[19] We are cut off from the epiphanies that keep our souls awake and breathing, trapped in a life-diminishing prison of ugliness.

Exposure to beauty is not a cure-all for traumatized and battered souls, but it is an essential component of holistic healing. Medicine can unlock our brains from debilitating conditions, but beauty can draw us into healthy attachments. Analytical modes of therapy can help dismantle false narratives and nurture new ones, but beauty can awaken new desires and loves. Patitsas writes, "the healing of the soul begins with noticing God's many theophanies and with falling in love with them. In other words, it begins with the eros of Beauty. In renewing our love for authentic Beauty . . . our character, unraveled by what we have experienced, begins to be knit together and becomes whole again."[20] We need beauty to breathe and be fully alive.

People suffer miserably for lack of many things, the most obvious being basic physiological and psychological health. But even if our basic needs are met, we can still suffer miserably from inattentiveness to the everyday epiphanies of God's beauty. As Abigail Carroll witnesses in her poem "What Men Die For Lack Of," we can get healing breaths of beauty from ordinary things like "a globed fruit, palpable and mute" or "telephone poles holding out their arms to birds" or "magenta pokeweed sprung in a vacant lot."[21]

The beauty that heals, however, is not merely pleasant, harmonious, luminous, or proportionate. If we conceive of beauty this way, it would be tempting to think that the healing journey involves complete removal from situations and experiences of dissonance, darkness, and disorderedness. By contrast, beauty is, as David Bentley Hart observes, "something mysterious, prodigal, often unanticipated, even capricious. We can find ourselves suddenly amazed by some strange and indefinable glory in a barren field, an urban ruin, the splendid disarray of a storm-wracked forest, and so on."[22] We can encounter beauty within emptiness and fullness, loss and gain, grief and joy.

Part of the latent beauty of a "storm-wracked forest" is its impending regeneration. The destruction of large trees creates room for smaller trees to grow. Fallen logs decay and become fertile ground for new life. Sunlight reaches parts of the forest floor previously shaded by the canopy. Forest fires do something similar. What looks like permanent destruction creates ideal conditions for new growth: annihilation of invasive species, ash-enriched soil, heat-induced seed germination. The vibrant green of new plant growth emerging amidst charred trunks and blackened earth may be one of the most beautiful scenes in nature. It's a reminder that death is an ending but also a new beginning, that new creation emerges out of the old. This is the kind of beauty that nurtures hope instead of despair.

⌀

Kathryn Alexander makes a compelling apologetic: "Our capacity for beauty might be our strongest ally in environmental work."[23] Beauty sustains our hope and therefore the belief that our labor—everything from earth-tending to art-making—is not in vain.[24]

⌀

Art doesn't need to aim at hope to be hopeful. While I think Ta-Nehisi Coates is right to warn us about sentimentality and feel-good art, I think he misses this critical undercurrent.[25] Even when an artist is not intending to communicate anything hopeful, the very act of making something new challenges despair. A work of art encounters us with new mixtures of sounds, new combinations of colors, new sequences of words, and new amalgamations of movements. Human artistry is not creation out of nothing (*creatio ex nihilo*) but creation out of anything (*creatio ex aliquo*), a fashioning of something new out of what currently is. Art is a testimony to the possibility of newness *no matter what*. Artistry and human creativity are living, breathing alternatives to ultimate tragedy.

Here's how Wendy Farley puts it: "The very act of creation is a refusal to accept tragedy as final. Creativity, perhaps paradoxically, allows us to grieve and lament even as it testifies—by its very existence—to the remnant that survives."[26] John W. de Gruchy makes a similar observation in his thoughtful study on art and transformation: "But even when [art] reflects despair, art expresses the human urge to creativity, and as such it is indicative of the hope that continually seeks to break through into human consciousness."[27] To create something is to trust that the future can be different and better than the past.

In her book *This Beautiful Truth*, Sarah Clarkson tells the story of Vedran Smailovic, a cellist who gained notoriety for playing Albinoni's "Adagio in G Minor" in the ruins of a downtown Sarajevo market following a brutal attack. He didn't just play it once, but repeated it over and over, for twenty-two consecutive days. Clarkson writes, "Straddling debris, balanced between wreckage, he drew his bow and filled those aching ruins with music." He didn't deny the existence of suffering and death, but "he defied death with a song." Those who gathered to listen or heard stories of the event afterward wondered, as Clarkson writes, "if beauty really could redeem a brutalized world."[28]

What if? This little, marvelous, open-ended question contains the power to transform how we orient our lives. Rather than a future full of locked doors, *what if?* entertains the possibility that at least one of the doors may be open and lead into a new reality. Trauma cramps our imaginations, so we only see the repetition of what has been and still is, whereas beauty stirs our imaginations to wonder *what if?* This suspension of disbelief gives space for us to breathe, even if we don't know how long the oxygen will last.

Wonder and beauty are not precise cures for disillusionment, but they certainly can stave off the despair of it.
To reclaim the awe of our child-selves, to allow ourselves
to be taken by the beauty of a thing, allows goodness to
take up the space it's often denied in our interior worlds.
                        —Cole Arthur Riley, *This Here Flesh*[29]

Children are naturally better than adults at wondering *what if?*
and also imagining *as if*: playing with this stick *as if* it were a
lightsaber, caring for these dolls *as if* they needed food, navigating the room *as if* it were filled with lava.[30] One of my favorite
animated television shows, *The Stinky & Dirty Show*, tapped
into this innate ability for kids to ask *what if?* and channeled
it toward creative problem solving.[31] Each episode featured
a garbage truck (Stinky) and a backhoe loader (Dirty) who
overcame a problem by asking *what if?* and imagining a way
forward. One day, after my son and I watched this show (confession: I may like this show more than he does and convince
him to watch it instead of *Power Rangers*), he turned to me
and asked: "What if Stinky and Dirty were real? Do you think
they'd clean up my room?" "It's possible," I replied, "but I bet
they would like help. What if you joined them up there now?"
Wondering *what if?* can be a subtle way of shirking responsibil-
ity, but at its best, it strengthens us to embrace responsibilities
when they seem too much to handle.

What if? can also feed anxiety and feel like little creatures
that crawl inside your ears at night to ask terrible questions, as

Shel Silverstein imagines in his poem "Whatif": "Whatif I'm dumb at school? Whatif they've closed the swimming pool? Whatif I get beat up? Whatif there's poison in my cup?"[32] And on and on it can go. Both beauty and ugliness entice us to wonder *what if?*, but the solution is not to shut down the imagination, but to open it up even wider to beautiful possibilities. What if goodness triumphs over evil? What if, despite all the trouble, God is making all things new? What if I spent more time doubting my doubts?

The arts are a gift for battered souls because they enable us to imagine new possibilities, move us to wonder *what if?*, and motivate us to live in hope. When Jesus began his public ministry, declaring good news and providing hope to those weary from centuries of waiting and battered by the Roman Empire, his preferred method of communication was parables and metaphors. The kingdom of God is like a mustard seed, like yeast, like a hidden treasure, like a net, like a banquet with the most unlikely people. By using this artful form of communication, Jesus helped his hearers imagine the now-and-not-yet reality of God's presence and kingdom. By telling the truth slant through stories and images, Jesus helps listeners in every culture imagine a new economy, a new reality, and a new family in which the last are first and the first are last. As we inhabit these stories, we are invited to see a new kingdom emerging within the shadow of brutal empire, heaven and earth merging now and into eternity. Art can reveal brokenness and get us in touch with all that needs to be restored, and it can also surprise us with delight and remind us of our deepest longings.

Even those who are still considering Jesus's claims will find a grounding for justice work in the cultivation of beauty. An encounter with beauty can show us what could be, and can make us rightly dissatisfied with the way things are.

—Makoto Fujimura, *Culture Care*[33]

Some will dismiss this emphasis on *what ifs* and hope and longing as the stuff of fairy tales. As Ta-Nehisi Coates concludes, "*The Burghers of Calais* don't need to smile for me. And I don't need *Macbeth* to be a fairy tale. Even our fairy tales are rarely fairy tales."[34] And yet, perhaps fairy tales exist not because of wishful, sentimental thinking but because happy endings are just as real as (if not more real than) tragic ones. If that's true, then fairy tales introduce us to the way things really are: broken but capable of repair beyond what we could ever imagine.

Can you imagine God coming to dwell with us, wiping away every tear, banishing death forever? Can you imagine life without mourning, crying, or pain?

Can you imagine the old order of things passing away to reveal a new heavens and new earth?

Can you imagine everything made new?[35]

The consolation of fairy-stories, the joy of the happy ending; or more correctly of the good catastrophe, the sudden joyous "turn" (for there is no true end to any fairy-tale): this joy, which is one of the things which fairy-stories can produce supremely well, is not essentially "escapist," nor "fugitive." In its fairy-tale—or otherworld—setting, it is a sudden and miraculous grace: never to be counted on to recur. It does not deny the existence of *dyscatastrophe*, of sorrow and failure: the possibility of these is necessary to the joy of deliverance; it denies (in the face of much evidence, if you will) universal final defeat and in so far is *evangelium*, giving a fleeting glimpse of Joy, Joy beyond the walls of the world, poignant as grief.

—J. R. R. Tolkien, "On Fairy-Stories"[36]

Also amazing—by which I mean gracious, surprising, wonderfully inexplicable—is how the Joy and Beauty beyond this world are constantly breaking into and permeating the world we inhabit. This is the joyful Beauty we observe in a camellia that remains seemingly dormant most of the year only to explode suddenly in fuchsia blooms in November, when everything else is descending into dreariness. This is the beautiful Joy in observing garlic we planted by faith during the last warm days of October and whose tender green shoots remain alive through all the frosts and snows and negligence, multiplying the underground cloves into a bulb that will emerge plump and pungent from the warm May soil. This is the joyful Beauty of a baby who develops from microscopic organism to fully formed human being in a mere nine months, which I realize does not in any way seem "mere" to the pregnant mother but is nevertheless a remarkable thing to happen in that span of time, not to mention how the mother's body then opens to release the baby into this bright world! All these beautiful and ordinary wonders remind us how, as Hopkins writes, "the Holy Ghost over the bent / World broods with warm breast and with ah! bright wings."[37]

The world is beautiful not just because it hauntingly reminds us of its creator, but also because it is pointing forward: it is designed to be filled, flooded, drenched with God.

—N. T. Wright, *Surprised by Hope*[38]

During the Covid-19 pandemic, our church community was feeling haggard and battered on many fronts. We needed hope. We needed more beauty in our lives, so we created a collaborative art piece called *Ebenezer for a Pandemic*, with a nod to the hymn "Come, Thou Fount of Every Blessing."[39] We asked anyone in the congregation to drop off or send in items that represented hope in their lives during lockdown: seed packets, notes from friends, sketches, poems, photos of bird nests, newspaper clippings, to-do lists, Scripture verses, dried flowers, and more. One of the artists in our community then assembled all the items into a collage, a colorful mishmash of materials evoking individual and communal perseverance, creativity, and joy. To riff off "Come, Thou Fount," this work of art reminded us that we are daily debtors to beauty that binds our wandering hearts to the God of hope.

Another thing our family did during the pandemic was discover all the nature preserves in our urban county. What hidden treasures! When the whole world was sheltering at home, even thirty minutes of sheltering under the shade of loblolly pines and walking through a grove of gigantic American beech trees was a refuge for our souls. In my experience, not only does the beauty of creation have a soothing, healing impact on my mind and body, but it also changes my frame of reference and shifts my questions. "Consider how the wild flowers grow," said Jesus. "They do not labor or spin. Yet I tell you, not even Solomon in all his splendor was dressed like one of these. If that is how God clothes the grass of the field, which is here today, and tomorrow is thrown into the fire, how much more will he clothe you—you of little faith!"[40]

My question: do I have what it takes to endure this?
God's answer: look at the flowers.
My question: why all this suffering?
God's answer: where were you when I laid the earth's foundation?[41]
My question: how can I navigate this heartache?
God's answer: have you ever given orders to the morning?[42]

God did not diminish what Job suffered, but there was God's aching request for Job to behold the kind of beauty that allowed him to live in the tension between God's power and his own suffering, to trust that beauty, to let it speak to him of God's tenderness and power, to walk forward into the wild country of trust . . . what if, in the bent and twisted darkness of our broken world, beauty is God's theodicy?

—Sarah Clarkson, *This Beautiful Truth*[43]

What if beauty will lead me home?
What if beauty can breathe life into these dry bones?
What if beauty is enough?

CHAPTER 6

Boredom and the Ache for Beauty

I n March of 2014, musician Father John Misty premiered his single "Bored in the USA" on the *Late Show with David Letterman*. This song criticizes the so-called American dream in a different way than Bruce Springsteen's 1984 hit "Born in the U.S.A." Whereas Springsteen laments the economic hardships of Vietnam veterans and related paradoxes of American militarism and patriotism, Father John Misty sardonically bemoans mindless days, meaningless consumerism, noncommittal relationships, useless education, mounds of debt, and overmedicated lives, all of which contribute to and result from being "bored in the USA." Feigning religious sincerity, he calls on both "white Jesus" and "President Jesus" to save him, obviously to no avail. As the song crescendos, so does the laugh track, but Father John Misty neither cracks a smile nor changes his tone. Is this intended as nervous laughter? Is it trying to show how humor is our feeble, last-ditch effort to deal with boredom? Whatever the intention, this is arguably one of the best—by which I mean saddest—artistic presentations of the buffered, bored self and the accompanying malaise. It shows that when all pride for being born in the USA disappears, what's left is boredom.

⌀

There is a difference, it seems to me, between boredom and Boredom.[1] One the one hand, boredom is not knowing what to do or the feeling that there is nothing interesting or engaging to do. Usually, children express boredom when they sulk into the room and declare "I'm BORED!!!" for all to hear, often accompanied with flopping on the floor like a dying fish (please don't tell me this only happens in my home). Adults can feel boredom as well, but we tend to be better at alleviating (hiding? avoiding?) it by doing *something*, even if that something involves turning on a glowing screen for distraction. This habit, of course, decreases our tolerance for boredom, training our brains to loathe it and relieve it as soon as possible.

On the other hand, Boredom is a state of soul-weariness stemming from the failure to find any meaning or purpose in life. This kind of Boredom is closely related to disillusionment but is less a clinical condition and more of a spiritual and existential one. But because things are rarely so simple, depression can intersect and overlap with Boredom and a sense of meaninglessness and spiritual apathy. In short, boredom may come and go, but Boredom tends to linger in our souls. Could it be that attention to beauty can help us deal with both boredom and Boredom?

According to Richard Beck, Boredom is a product of disenchantment. Without any sense of transcendence, mystery, or porousness, life becomes aimless and flat, and the best we can do is live for ourselves and acquire as much stuff and experiences as we can, a strategy that may work for a time but is ultimately unsatisfying and dull. In other words: "Boredom is the price of possessiveness. Monotony is the cost of acquiring and hoarding."[2]

People will say that boredom is productive, and many studies back that up.[3] Boredom can spur creativity, allow space for generative daydreaming, and give our brains time to rest and play. People will also say, Kierkegaard being one of them, that boredom—probably both boredom and Boredom—is the root of all evil.[4] Consequently, it's important to clarify what we're talking about when we talk about boredom. Some forms of boredom are generative, leading to fresh encounters with beauty, whereas other forms of Boredom are degenerative, perpetuating lack of receptivity, curiosity, and openness to the sheer wonder of things.

"Why is the self," asks novelist Walker Percy, "the only object in the cosmos which gets bored?" And why does this boredom and a sense of self-imprisonment only seem to be increasing in contemporary life despite "an ever heightened self-consciousness, increased leisure, ever more access to cultural and recreational facilities, ever more instruction on self-help, self-growth, self-enrichment?" Answer: "boredom is the self being stuffed with itself."[5]

When I was a kid, admitting to boredom within earshot of my parents would lead to an eager review of the to-do list, which was always miraculously replenished, much like the widow's jar of flour, although not delightfully miraculous in this case.[6] "If you're bored, there are plenty of jobs for you!" This parental declaration was sometimes accompanied by nostalgic reference to a boredom-less, hard-working childhood, worn like a badge of honor: "When we were kids, we didn't have time to be bored . . . there were too many mouths to feed." (Confession: I may have used similar but less convincing and ultimately unsuccessful rhetoric with my own kids, the lack of success surely owing to my hypocritical adoption of this strategy.) In this view, boredom may not be the root of all evil, but it is resolutely *not* something that will put food on the table or keep the house clean and beautiful.

Work is a typical American way to deal with boredom, as unsuccessful as the approach may be. One survey indicated that more than two-thirds of American workers experience boredom on a daily basis, many of them expressing an overall sense of boredom with their jobs. Cue the scene from *The Office* where Jim stares straight ahead at his desk, his body slowly crumpling forward until his head hits the desk, followed by Pam's commentary: "Every so often, Jim dies of boredom. I think today it was the expense reports that did him in."[7]

Boredom is like dust. You go about and never notice, you breathe it in, you eat and drink it. It is sifted so fine, it doesn't even grind on your teeth. Stand still for an instant and there it is, coating your face and hands. To shake off this drizzle of ashes you must be forever on the go. And so people are always "on the go."

—Georges Bernanos,
The Diary of a Country Priest[8]

97

O

Busyness may be a convenient way to deal with boredom—"to shake off the drizzle of ashes"—but what happens when busyness itself is boring? Maybe more busyness will help?! More consumption. More products. More entertainment. Yet with more busyness comes more boredom comes more busyness comes more boredom, and the vicious, unsatisfying cycle continues. Life becomes less and less breathable.

Four centuries ago, Blaise Pascal observed how we seek consolation from our misery in diversion and yet how diversion becomes our great misery: "All our life passes in this way: We seek rest by struggling against certain obstacles, and once they are overcome, rest proves intolerable because of the boredom it produces. We must get away from it and crave excitement."[9]

Many churches have bought into the boredom-busyness cycle as the new normal, laboring to offer consolations and resources to busy-bored people rather than proclaiming genuine good news that obliterates the cycle by offering deep rest and liberation from an achievement-oriented life.[10] To do so, however, would entail challenging the never-ending need for acceleration, a vision of busyness as the essence of the good life, and a jam-packed, active life as the antidote to boredom.

What we really need, argues Andrew Root, is a different kind of fullness. We need the fullness of interconnection, resonance, and mystery. We need the fullness of beauty.[11] This kind of fullness, however, cannot be achieved by doing more, having more, or being more. It arrives as a gift. We won't find the antidote to boredom by being on the go or by staying on the treadmill of continuous and exhausting activity. We'll find a way to breathe again by becoming unbusy, by waiting, by cultivating a readiness for beauty, wonder, and surprise.

Like Inigo Montoya in *The Princess Bride*, however, we hate waiting, especially with technology and turbo capitalism conditioning us to experience waiting as bad and unnecessary. In 2018, Delta Airlines launched their "runway" advertising campaign featuring people enjoying scintillating experiences around the globe, confirming that waiting is for losers and "good things come to those who go."[12] This stands in contrast to the Heinz commercials of my childhood, which celebrated "the best things come to those who wait," including thick ketchup out of hefty glass bottles. But even those commercials situated the expectant, waiting person in a nostalgic past, framing the capacity to wait as a characteristic of "the good ol' days" instead of the edgy 1980s. Looking back now at the 1980s and early 90s, it's hard to imagine waiting for that squealing, dial-up internet connection.

Waiting is one of the most frequently modeled and commended postures in the biblical story. In the slow story of a slow God, waiting is the nature of the journey: waiting for the Messiah, waiting for the fulfillment of God's covenant promises, waiting for answers to prayer,[13] waiting for the goodness of the Lord in the land of the living,[14] waiting for redemption,[15] waiting for Jesus to return,[16] waiting for a new heavens and new earth,[17] waiting for God's glory to be revealed.[18] As Root reminds us, "this waiting is not inactive, not a slumped cocoon of boredom or listlessness."[19] Waiting is a receptive posture that enables genuine encounters with beauty here and now as a foretaste of the fullness of beauty yet to come.

Some of my most visceral experiences of waiting have occurred in tree stands during hunting season.[20] Sitting alone in the woods, enduring freezing temperatures, and waiting for deer to walk by may seem like the epitome of boredom, but for me the opposite is true. While I admit to suffering through some miserably cold mornings, it is hard to be bored when surrounded by so much beauty: mice scuttling through underbrush, elaborate moss formations on oak trees, nuthatches flitting from trunk to trunk, leaves floating down and adding patches of color to the forest carpet. One time a chickadee flew from a nearby tree and landed on the barrel of my rifle, taking a moment to fluff its feathers and study me before flying off to a more amenable branch. Another time two pine martens scampered into view, spending what seemed like an eternity chasing each other up one tree and down another. As I later learned, pine marten mating season is in the summer months, so it seems what I witnessed was a playful game of chase. In my experience, beauty comes to those who wait.

The conundrum of many bored souls is not knowing what all the waiting is for. Like Vladimir and Estragon in Samuel Beckett's play, many of us are "waiting for Godot"; but we don't know who that is, when this person is coming, or why we are waiting in the first place. We hurry up to wait but waiting makes us think we should be on the go. But to where?

> Estragon: Well, shall we go?
> Vladimir: Yes, let's go.
> *They do not move.*
> *Curtain.*[21]

While *Waiting for Godot* is a play about meaninglessness and the futility of waiting, it also invites the audience to consider the role of aesthetic experience within a life of boredom. Was this two-hour theatrical experience merely a temporary escape from our own boring lives? In *A Philosophy of Boredom*, Lars Svendsen doubts that aesthetic experience can ultimately alleviate our boredom, given the short-lived satisfaction it offers. "As long as the music lasts, we escape boredom, but, sooner or later, the music will stop."[22] If there is a solution to boredom, remarks Svendsen, it has something to do with transcendence, since "boredom is immanence in its purest form." But "how can transcendence be possible within an immanence?"[23] In the end, Svendsen concludes that the problem of boredom lacks a solution.[24] Within the immanent frame, it's seemingly impossible to experience transcendent beauty within mundane aesthetic experience. But what if one could? Might boredom create a readiness for renewed astonishment?

A common way to deal with boredom is to keep creating and innovating, but that may or may not have anything to do with beauty. For buffered souls, creativity is not always a faithful response to the beauty of God; it is sometimes a way to keep boredom at bay and fuel the busyness.[25] Human creativity severed from the reality of divine creativity becomes another futile attempt to gain mastery over the world rather than enjoying our immersion within it. Creativity can become another form of stifling monotony that pursues what's newer and better and faster, like the latest mobile phone release.

Monotony can be either soul-*stifling* or soul-*stirring*. Crunching numbers in a cubicle may be soul-*stifling* monotony for some and a soul-*stirring* vocation for others. Hiking the Appalachian Trail, putting one foot in front of another for miles on end, could either be soul-*stifling* monotony or a soul-*stirring* adventure depending on your health, perspective, and purpose. Repeatedly going over the same drills in soccer practice might feel like soul-*stifling* monotony, whereas kicking a soccer ball over and over with a six-year-old can feel like soul-*stirring* monotony, at least to the child, for whom each kick produces more pleasure than the previous one. As Chesterton noted, a child "always says, 'Do it again,' and the grown-up person does it again until he is nearly dead. For grown-up people are not strong enough to exult in monotony." Monotony itself is not the problem, but rather our failure to encounter beauty in and through monotony. After all, monotonous laws and processes—through which, I might add, God goes belonging—are how this beautiful world is sustained. As such, "The repetition in Nature may not be mere recurrence; it may be a theatrical encore."[26] The least we can do is stand up and clap along with creation.

> You will go out in joy
>   and be led forth in peace;
> the mountains and hills
>   will burst into song before you,
> and all the trees of the field
>   will clap their hands.
>
> —Isaiah 55:12

Monotony is the most beautiful or the most atrocious thing. The most beautiful if it is a reflection of eternity. The most atrocious if it is the sign of an unvarying perpetuity. It is time surpassed or time sterilized. The circle is the symbol of monotony which is beauty, the swinging of a pendulum, monotony which is atrocious.

—Simone Weil, *Gravity and Grace*[27]

Modern American life is obsessed with the pendulum of time and managing how we "spend" each tick and tock. "Time management" is the secret to navigating a fast life with efficiency and control. In this lifestyle, beauty becomes a means toward achieving what Wendell Berry calls "the objective," which is "the destruction of all enemies . . . the destruction of all obstacles . . . to clear the way to victory . . . to clear the way to promotion, to salvation, to progress."[28] We may think that keeping our eyes fixed on this objective of upward mobility will lead to the good life, but instead it generates atrocious monotony, the boredom and sense of homelessness that results from what Berry calls "self-realization." What if beauty is not the means toward another objective but is the longed-for end, the real objective of our lives? And if beauty comes to those who wait, then a beauty-oriented life requires habits of slowness: availability, attention, stillness, patience, quality-over-quantity.[29]

Hartmut Rosa connects the fast life with experiences of alienation, which is another word to describe the ache of bored souls.[30] Alienation is a lack of meaningful, vibrant, resonant connection with others and the world, or as Rosa describes it, experiencing physical and social interactions as "external, unconnected, nonresponsive, in a word: mute."[31] These alienating, joyless interactions are most common when we rush through life without breathing in beauty. Within the busyness of contemporary life, it is increasingly common to experience alienation with creation, one's body, the workplace, home life, in relationship with others, and in connection with religious practices. How do we recover the vibrancy and aliveness of these relationships and spheres of life?

Familiarity can breed boredom and alienation because we can get so used to any given person, place, or thing that it loses its luster, uniqueness, agency, and mystery. We lose touch with its beauty. Robert Farrar Capon writes about how we can regain the wonder of an ordinary practice like slicing an onion, and I think his method can apply to most anything.[32]

First, savor the otherness of the onion and the uniqueness of the moment, the place, and this "mutual confrontation." Second, look at the onion "as if you had never seen an onion before," meeting it on its own terms. When you do so, you'll realize that it's not a sphere, but "a bloom of vectors thrusting upward from base to tip." Third, peel off the outer layer of onion skin and consider the "elegant and deliberate dryness" of it that protects the watery interior. Fourth, cut the onion in half and look at the stunning result: "You have opened the floodgates of being." Observe the structure, colors, moisture, pressure, and smell, that "noble reek" released from its interior. Fifth, remove each section of the onion intact, beginning with the heart, and line them up by size on the table to observe these light, rigid, and crisp "tongues of fire." Sixth, pick up a piece and cut it lengthwise in strips, blinking the tears from your eyes and listening carefully to the "audible response of cellularity." Finally, take a sliver and squeeze, press, and roll it until all the water comes out; then you'll discover "the deepest revelation of all:" the onion has basically disappeared.

As it turns out, the whole onion was "an aqueous house of cards" animated by the same water that constitutes all living beings, the water God created and called very good. This whole exercise may seem over the top, but if you do it, I promise your relationship with onions will no longer be boring, alienating, or mute. Sometimes beauty stings your eyes. If you repeat a similar exercise of focused attention and slow appreciation with any familiar person, place, or thing, I think you'll be surprised by your capacity for delight and how the world can come utterly alive.

Hartmut Rosa's proposed antidote to alienation is articulate and complex, but it matches what Capon suggests for our relationship with an onion: attentiveness to the uniqueness, agency, and beauty of all that is other, and an openness to resonant relationships.[33] Rather than hurrying through our environments in detached ways, we should pause long enough to notice the beauty and strangeness of familiar places. Rather than interacting with people as if we already knew them, we should approach each interaction with a posture of curiosity, discovery, and anticipation. Rather than merely consuming art and culture that satisfies our preferences, we should foster a willingness to engage with new and surprising expressions.

Rather than approaching God for answers, we should begin with humble astonishment. There is a breathable life beyond boredom, but it's easy to get stuck in monotonous grooves.

I resonate with Annie Dillard's admission: "Beauty is real. I would never deny it; the appalling thing is that I forget it."[34] Drift happens. Things go mute. Relationships shift to neutral and lose their resonance. The earth and its creatures become "flat, uniform, monochrome," no longer inciting wonder and curiosity.[35] Sometimes, I just need to slow down, get unbusy, and learn to pay attention and be astonished.[36]

The work that Mary Oliver embraced as a poet is a fitting mission for us all, "which is mostly standing still and learning to be astonished."[37]

CHAPTER 7

The Beautiful Ordinary

As I write this, it's currently the beginning of Ordinary Time, the portion of the church calendar outside the "special" seasons of Advent, Christmastide, Lent, and Eastertide. Contrary to the usual meaning of "ordinary," the thirty-three (sometimes thirty-four) weeks of Ordinary Time are not meant to be less special than other seasons. "Ordinary" refers to the method of using *ordinal* numbers to distinguish the weeks—first, second, third, etc.—for this season and way of experiencing time. Unfortunately, the common definition of "ordinary" conditions me to feel more humdrum and meh about this time of year than others. I automatically associate Ordinary Time with less excitement, less anticipation, and less beauty. But this is simply untrue. God's beauty belongs to the ordinary just as much as the extraordinary, just as God incarnate inhabited the ordinary Nazareth years as well as the special years of public ministry.[1] Ordinary times, places, people, and objects may seem boring at times, but I've come to see them as the primary context for receiving beauty as oxygen for my soul.

A little trail meanders through the woods behind my office. When the trail is not too soggy from recent rain, I enjoy a short walk after lunch. Sometimes if I'm slow and attentive, I will spot a white-tailed deer, and we will stare at each other for a few intense seconds before it bounds out of sight. But most of the time it's just me, the trees and grasses, the birds, and the spiders, which love to spin webs across the trail. One time, the sunlight glinted off a web, preventing me from crashing through it, and I found a marbled orbweaver enjoying its silky retreat. Appropriately named, the abdomen on this spider is orange with black marbling, making it look like a carved pumpkin. On other walks, I have stumbled upon other spiders with different but equally astonishing colorations, and thus I find myself, like Jonathan Edwards, "conversant with spiders" as I go marveling through these ordinary moments.[2] Boredom begins to dissolve in encountering all this beauty.

I resonate with Mary Oliver's experience of each day encountering something that "kills me with delight." These things are rarely "the exceptional, the fearful, the dreadful, the very extravagant," but rather "the ordinary, the common, the very drab, the daily presentations." We were born to lose ourselves in this beauty, "the untrimmable light of the world."[3]

Radical is the sort of word many Christians like.[4] Radical faith. Radical church. Radical discipleship. Radical mission. But I wonder if radical faith is the correct antidote to a boring, stale faith. Before offering some criticism, let me acknowledge that there *is* something radical about Jesus's call to follow him.[5] Etymologically, *radical* comes from the Latin *radix*, meaning *root*, and understood that way, radical faith is simply faith that takes root in good soil and bears fruit.[6] That being said, the call to be radical can—whether intentionally or unintentionally—denigrate the significance of the ordinary. Faith requires commitment; it comes with a cost. But what if part of the cost is to abandon entitlement to an extraordinary life? One of the most radical lifestyles is to stay rooted and attentive to beauty within the ordinary.[7]

Another thing some Christians like to talk about is how God "showed up." Usually, testimonies of this kind highlight surprising situations and interactions that turn out for the good because of God's arrival. While I appreciate the desire to identify divine action within the mundane, I wonder if the idea of "God showing up" gets it backward. Instead of celebrating how God showed up, what if we celebrated times when we showed up to the God who is already there? In our busyness and inattentiveness, it's easy to miss how God is already at work or assume that God is active only when we see tangible benefits. But surely if God in Christ by the Spirit is holding all things together and sustaining all things by his powerful word,[8] then the fundamental requirement is to show up and pay attention to all the ways God's beauty already permeates this world.

Without the pressure of wondering when God will show up, the journey through ordinary time becomes what John O'Donohue calls "an adventure in beauty." It's a journey of reverence and discovery, and rather than suffering the endless cycle of boredom and busyness, you can "take your time and be everywhere you are."[9]

That's easier said than done, of course. It's one thing to be fully present and attentive to beauty on a walk in the woods or during a night out at a jazz club. It is quite another to do so while changing the seventh dirty diaper of the day, writing yet another email, battling an illness, or navigating a wounded relationship. All of us have challenges, some more intense and difficult than others, that make availability and attentiveness to beauty an uphill battle. Within that struggle, it is fitting to think of wonder like your diaphragm, a muscle that keeps the lungs of your soul breathing in beauty. Letting wonder atrophy makes the battle even harder.

Rachel Carson shares that if she were a magical fairy, she would give to all children "a sense of wonder so indestructible that it would last throughout life, as an unfailing antidote to boredom and disenchantments of later years, sterile preoccupation with things that are artificial, the alienation from sources of strength."[10]

Since we can't count on a magical fairy to show up, we need to cultivate habits of wonder that will see us through times of disenchantment. Breath prayer is one such practice for me, because it creates a holy pause in my day and increases my capacity for wonder. For example, before going into a meeting, I might pause for a breath prayer:

> Inhale: Attune my senses
> Exhale: To the beauty of this meeting.

This prayer helps me show up to the meeting not as a task-master but as a beauty beholder and "beauty chaser."[11] It doesn't necessarily mean that the coworker who annoyed me last meeting will miraculously cease to be annoying or that the conversation will be fascinating. But it does help me walk into the room with more wonder, attentive to the beauty of my fellow human beings, our ways of interacting, and to the energy of the Spirit in our midst. You can use a similar breath prayer at any transition in your day.

> Inhale: Attune my senses
> Exhale: To the beauty of this moment.

We need training to expect beauty in mundane moments and small things because we live in a culture that celebrates the large, splashy, and exceptional. American playwright Sarah Ruhl surmises that delight in small and ordinary things may be the secret to our transformation: "Smallness is subversive, because smallness can creep into smaller places and wreak transformation at the most vulnerable, cellular level. In a time when largeness is threatening to topple us, I wish to remember and praise the beauty of smallness, in order to banish the Goliath of loneliness."[12]

Another wonder habit is simply going outside and paying attention. Whenever I complained of boredom as a kid, my parents would send me outside, and I utilize the same strategy with my own kids. The point is not merely to create distance from their whining, although that can be a mercy, but to put them in proximity to beauty. It doesn't always work, since they are just as capable of pouting outside as inside, but often their wonder muscles start working and their moods improve. Overturned rocks reveal bugs to collect for the front porch museum (admission $1). Vine-tangled thickets in the alley invite exploration and transform into an impenetrable castle (no boys allowed). Shifting clouds look delightfully like rabbits and unicorns (What else do you see?).

Speaking of clouds, did you know there is such a thing as the Cloud Appreciation Society and they even have a manifesto? "We believe that clouds are unjustly maligned and that life would be immeasurably poorer without them. . . . Life would be dull if we had to look up at cloudless monotony day after day. . . . We believe that clouds are for dreamers and their contemplation benefits the soul."[13]

> Stop in your tracks! Take in God's
>   miracle-wonders!
> Do you have any idea how God does it all,
> how he makes bright lightning from dark
>   storms,
> How he piles up the cumulus clouds—
> all these miracle-wonders of a perfect Mind?
>   —Job 37:14–16 (*The Message*)

Clouds are commendable for cultivating wonder because you don't even need to be outside to gaze at them. Right now, as I sit at my desk, a sheet of altostratus clouds drifts slowly through the sky, creating the best kind of day-dreamy distraction. Fabiana Fondevila says it well: "We don't want to look at clouds to divine the weather forecast; we want to look at them so that we can dream again and remember that magic and beauty surrounds us at every step. We want to find in them a route back into wonder."[14] Clouds tell a story more wondrous than the weather.

Most people love a good story, partly because our brains are hardwired for story but also because life itself has a narrative shape, structured by a beginning, middle, and end, and filled with conflict in search of resolution. Despite our inherent love for stories, the challenges of buffered, battered, and bored existence can easily deplete the wonder we feel about our own stories and the stories that surround us. Buffered souls find it difficult to believe in a grand, sacred story beyond the machinations of self-interest. Battered souls struggle to imagine how real stories can have a happy ending or genuine joy along the way. Bored souls lose motivation to look beyond the dullness of the moment for any story at all. Given these challenges, one of the most important ways to cultivate wonder within the ordinary is to read, hear, tell, and watch good stories. The stories we encounter, whether fictional or nonfictional, shape our imaginations, desires, and loves and therefore shape our lives. The question is not "Am I shaped by stories?" The real question is "What stories are and could be shaping me?"

0

Growing up I read a lot of the Hardy Boys, Louis L'Amour, and Gary Paulsen novels, all of which shaped me to imagine there is no mystery too thick for me to unravel, no problem too large for me to solve, and no wilderness too harsh for me to navigate (emphasis on *me*, and sometimes me and my brother). These convictions produced some positive benefits in my coming-of-age years but have ultimately proved false, especially in my relationship with God. Just by virtue of losing myself in these stories, however, I was being formed to see the beauty of setting, character, plot, conflict, and resolution, and not just in those stories, but in *my* story and the story of the world. Thankfully, my story-diet also included C. S. Lewis's *The Chronicles of Narnia* and his space trilogy, George MacDonald's *At the Back of the North Wind*, Wilson Rawls's *Where the Red Fern Grows*, and Alan Paton's *Cry, the Beloved Country*, filling my imagination with the reality of evil and the power of redemption.[15] They helped me realize that life is never boring, that beauty involves sacrifice, and that I'm called to be a witness rather than a hero.

Some people will argue that reading or watching fantasies, myths, and fairy tales is less productive than exposure to more "realistic" stories. Why immerse yourself in a fanciful story about a faraway world? Isn't that just an escape from the real world? Tolkien argued that fairy tales can indeed offer escape, but the kind of escape that enables us to recover a true view of ourselves and the reality of heaven and earth that so-called "realists" deny. After all, who gets to determine what is real? Tolkien contends, "Fairy-stories may invent monsters that fly the air or dwell in the deep, but at least they do not try to escape from heaven or the sea."[16] In doing so, these stories can help us recover a sense of wonder within the beautiful ordinary and can draw us out from self-preoccupation. "We need, in any case, to clean our windows; so that the things seen clearly may be freed from the drab blur of triteness or familiarity—from possessiveness."[17] What is more, fairy-stories show us how evil and beauty can exist side by side until the great *eucatastrophe*, the joyous consummation of the story.

The more we breathe in the beauty of good stories, the more we'll breathe out wonder and joy. As Timothy Willard writes, Joy is "our gasp at the beautiful."[18] Or as John O'Donohue observes, "We respond with joy to the call of beauty because in an instant it can awaken under the layers of the heart a forgotten brightness," a brightness dulled by boredom.[19]

Breath prayers, going outside and paying attention, enjoying good stories: these practices take time and intentionality. While it's possible and preferable to work them into daily rhythms, observing a weekly Sabbath day provides dedicated time and space to experience beauty. Sabbath is an invitation to say "No" to busyness and "Yes" to restful attentiveness. Sabbath is for delight. Norman Wirzba draws the connection between beauty, delight, and Sabbath, for "to take delight is finally to relish the goodness and beauty of God's work and to see in each other the trace of God."[20] Similarly, Dan Allender describes Sabbath as time to "enter a dance with God and others and experience a beauty that takes our breath away."[21] Beauty takes our breath away in wonder only to give it back again in praise.

It is good to praise the Lord
   and make music to your name,
      O Most High,
proclaiming your love in the morning
   and your faithfulness at night,
to the music of the ten-stringed lyre
   and the melody of the harp.
For you make me glad by your deeds, Lord;
   I sing for joy at what your hands have done.
      —Psalm 92:1–4, a song for the Sabbath

The works of God's hands include all the ordinary and extraordinary ways God's beauty is displayed: a jug of lemonade and a jagged mountain landscape, a bluebird in the bleak midwinter and iridescent northern lights, the uniqueness of each glittering snowflake and each human personality, an embrace from a child and how the sea both hugs and pummels the shore, a sugar maple on fire with fall color and a bush burning on divine command, the law of gravity and the law given at Sinai, the release of winter into spring and the liberation of an enslaved people, the metamorphosis of a caterpillar into a butterfly and the transformation of cracked icons into glorious images of God. The beautiful work of God's hands incites our praise.

    Praise is the culmination of wonder and delight. Lewis explains how "praise not merely expresses but completes the enjoyment: it is its appointed consummation." It is disheartening and unfitting, for example, "to come suddenly, at the turn of the road, upon some mountain valley of unexpected grandeur and then to have to keep silent because the people with you care for it no more than a tin can in a ditch."[22] Praise—whether in casual conversation, private prayer, or corporate worship—is an essential practice for ongoing wonder and enjoyment, especially because, as Lewis notes, the reasons for praise are never-ending. One of the reasons Christians gather to worship every week is because our diaphragm of wonder gets all knotted up; it needs to be released so we can breathe in beauty and exhale praise.

I've heard some people talk about nature as their church and hiking as their act of worship, and I get where they're coming from, especially if their church experience has been traumatic, misleading, or restrictive. But while enjoying the community of creation is indeed a worshipful experience, it doesn't replace gathering with the family of God for the ordinary yet beautiful practices of meeting, praising, praying, confessing, hearing, sharing, communing, and sending. Participating in the drama of corporate worship reminds us of where beauty comes from, how it gets ignored, twisted, and idolized, and how God is at work to make all things beautiful again. Corporate worship can open up the buffered soul, comfort the battered soul, and incite the bored soul toward wonder before the realities of grace and resurrection.

David Taylor shows how the liturgical arts have a formative role to play in the drama of corporate worship, not only in countering "the idols of the mind, the forgetfulness of memories, a will that is bent against God, and the disorder of broken bodies and dysfunctional emotions," but also in attuning our imaginations to the beauty of a triune God.[23]

Spontaneous wonder is a welcome experience, but cultivated and disciplined wonder is the real antidote to boredom and despair. The author of Hebrew writes: "Let us hold un-swervingly to the hope we profess, for he who promised is faithful. And let us consider how we may spur one another on toward love and good deeds, not giving up meeting together, as some are in the habit of doing, but encouraging one another—and all the more as you see the Day approaching."[24] What would it look like to cultivate wonder unswervingly? What if we spurred each other on toward the good deed of marveling? What if we committed to meeting and worshipping together for the sake of wonder?

Despite all its weaknesses and because of the powerful grace of God, the church is what Alejandro García-Rivera calls "the community of the beautiful." God's beauty permeates all of creation, but "the Glory of God is a community that has caught sight of a marvelous vision, a universe of justice emerging from a community's experience of divine Beauty."[25] The church is a beautiful community called to bring more beauty into the world by making disciples and making culture.[26]

In my experience, breathing in beauty inspires me to nurture it, sustain it, and create more of it. The work of God's hands inspires the work of mine. After encountering a magnificent magnolia tree, I'm inspired to plant one in our backyard. After experiencing the freshness of a spring morning, I'm moved to write a few lines of poetry. When the daffodils bloom along the garden fence, I'm motivated to cut some and arrange them, perhaps with some early shoots of Russian sage, on the dining room table. Beauty reminds me that I am created in God's image as a sub-creator.[27]

Beauty calls us to create. Before the breaking of the world, we were formed in the image of an artist God whose first acts in time were those of profound and beautiful creation. To be made in his image and redeemed by his love is, inescapably, to be called to creation. . . . Beauty bears God's life to us, but it always calls us, in turn, to bear the life of God to the rest of the broken world.

—Sarah Clarkson, *This Beautiful Truth*[28]

Not everyone is an artist, but everyone is creative. To deny our vocation to create is to diminish our humanity, for as Madeleine L'Engle wrote, "unless we are creators, we are not fully alive."[29] Another way out of boredom, therefore, is to embrace this call to create. Some people create symphonies; others create spreadsheets. Some people create houses; others create art that hangs on house walls. Some people create films; others create software that runs the cameras. To be human is to be creative and to join in God's creative mission to make all things new. What if we reimagined work as a response to beauty, an expression of our inherent creativity, a way to participate in the mystery of new creation through the work of our hands?

And let the beauty of the Lord our God be
upon us,

and establish the work of our hands for us;
yes, establish the work of our hands.

—Psalm 90:17 NKJV

Nothing is too ordinary to be beautiful, and no action is too ordinary to be creative. The work of your hands may not always seem significant in the grand scheme of things, but even the smallest task can be offered as a sacrifice of praise. Even the most mundane moments of eating and drinking are ways to breathe in beauty and glorify God.[30] Just as there are "no little people," so there are no little tasks.[31] Here are some worthy ways of bringing beauty into the world today, even if you knew Jesus were returning tomorrow:

Plant an apple tree.[32]

Bake cookies and bring some to a neighbor.

Bring your full self to work.

Weed a vegetable garden and eat some green beans right off the vine.

Make a pot of tea and invite a friend over.

Cozy up by a fire or in a hammock and read a book.

Let the kids crawl under the warm pile of laundry before folding it.

Go on a walk, leaving your phone at home.

Say your prayers, as well as plenty of *pleases* and *thank yous*.

"Plant sequoias . . . laugh . . . practice resurrection."[33]

Consider Abigail Carroll's suggestions for "how to prepare for the second coming":

> Start by recalling the absolute goodness of rain
> and repent for every grumble you have
>   ever made
> about the weather (this will take approximately
>
> forever.) . . .
> . . . . Teach a child to lace
> a shoe (your child or another's—any
>   four-year-old
>
> will do), and while you're at it, set the alarm
> for three, and fumble through the dark to
>   the pond
> to guard the salamanders as they cross
>   the road. . . .[34]

There is more than enough beauty in ordinary life to keep your soul breathing. Staying attentive to beauty can save your day from boredom. And if Annie Dillard is right that "how we spend our days is, of course, how we spend our lives," then staying attentive to beauty may, in the end, save your life.[35]

CHAPTER 8

What Sort of Beauty Will Save the World?

"The world will be saved by beauty." This famous declaration, attributed to Russian novelist Fyodor Dostoevsky, is often misunderstood. In the original context midway through Dostoevsky's novel *The Idiot*, the phrase appears as a question by which Ippolit confronts the protagonist, Prince Myshkin: "Is it true, Prince, that you said once that the world would be saved by 'beauty'?" Ippolit, a young atheist dying from tuberculosis, surmises that the Prince only believes in the salvific power of beauty because he is in love, but Ippolit tries again to procure an answer: "What sort of beauty will save the world?" The Prince never responds, letting the riddle of beauty's salvific power stand unanswered.[1]

I think Ippolit's revised question—what *sort* of beauty will save the world?—is the right one, for if beauty will indeed save the world, it needs to be a particular kind of beauty. Does a beauty that is *of* the world have the power to save it? Could it be that beauty has to be both beyond the world (transcendent) and in the world (immanent) to have salvific power? Our answers to these questions also depend on what it means for the world or anything in it to be saved. Saved from despair? Saved from decay or death itself? And what would beauty save the world *for*? A life of joy? An eternal existence of limitless beauty?

To begin, it is fitting to talk about the power of natural and artistic beauty to save us from a meaningless, despairing experience of this life. This is likely what Mary Oliver meant when she told Krista Tippett in an interview: "I got saved by poetry, and I got saved by the beauty of the world." Despite a difficult childhood, the beauty of woods and words gave Oliver's life purpose and inspired her to bring even more beauty into the world through her own literary creativity.[2]

For beauty to save in this way is to claim natural and artistic beauty as oxygen for a life of meaning and joy despite the challenges of buffered, battered, and bored existence. Beauty won't magically erase trauma and pain, but it can give strength for each day. Beauty won't eliminate injustice, but it can provide hope beyond current circumstances. Beauty won't ease all the tensions of a buffered life, but it can introduce a sense of wonder and enchantment as a bridge to the sacred. In this sense, beauty can "save" any person at any time, and every time it does, the world looks and feels a little bit brighter. The wonder incited by beauty, writes Cole Arthur Riley, "is a force of liberation."[3]

While my growing up years were free from the intense trauma many children experience, I did have moments when I needed the companionship of the woods. Behind our house was a trail that ran through a grove of bur oaks and a few towering red pines to the top of Scenic Slope, where a prominent chunk of granite served as a perfect spot to be alone and survey the surrounding ravines. It's hard to explain—but anyone who has a similar "spot" in nature will know what I mean—how healing that place was for me. It felt like home. It felt like freedom. It felt like oxygen for my soul when the rest of the world was closing in. It felt like being saved by beauty.

Artistic beauty can have a similar impact, especially in a context, as theologian Jason Goroncy writes, replete "with a growing recognition of unsettling contingency, the gnawing of dis-ease, the erosion of old certainties, and the despoilation of hope."[4] Goroncy is quick to point out that art is neither a messianic fix nor a panacea for "the greater demons of our nature," but it can provide at least "a point of departure, a way to not simply bandage the wounds of victims beneath the wheels of injustice, but rather to drive a lance or to even throw oneself into the spokes of the wheel itself."[5] Even if art can't save us or the world from ultimate demise, it can save us from apathy and resignation. Novelist and poet Erica Jong expresses the tension between what poetic beauty can and cannot do by admitting that "no poem will unwrite lawsuits, / unseat senator, or unbribe judges." No poem will ungrow cancer, yet we still "write poems / as leaves give oxygen / so we can breathe."[6]

A friend and church leader for whom I have deep love and respect broke his neck in a car accident early in his adult life and has lived with persistent pain and suffering for more than thirty years. Apart from the hope of bodily resurrection in Christ, the thing that most enables him to persevere is the presence of beauty amidst affliction. During a particularly difficult season for me in life and ministry, this friend would occasionally email me, reminding me that if we are attentive, some moments, interactions, scenes, and artistic expressions are so beautiful they can eclipse the affliction, at least for a time. Beauty may not unbreak my friend's neck, but it does bring healing to his soul along the way. Beauty may not unmake the difficulty of pastoral ministry or other challenging vocations, but it does make them more breathable.

Writer and publisher Gregory Wolfe acknowledges that although the beauty of made things may not be able to save our souls in an ultimate sense, "it can do much to redeem the time, to give us a true image of ourselves, both in the horror and the boredom to which we can descend, and in the glory which we may, in rare moments, be privileged to glimpse."[7]

If beauty can save a soul from despair, can it also save a soul from the curse of death? Most Christian theologians deny this possibility, especially if by *beauty* we mean the beauty of things created by God or made by humans. According to N. T. Wright, the beauty of created things cannot save us, but it is a "broken signpost" of the one who does.[8] Consequently, if we look to created beauty to save our souls rather than the Creator, we will be constantly dissatisfied and misled by idolatry. As Lewis argued, our longing for created beauty reveals our underlying desire for a distant country, one in which we will become the splendor we experience in the here and now.[9] Similarly, Chris

Green concludes that like all created things, "beauty, given or made, must be saved from itself and from us" in order to be given back to us as oxygen for our souls.[10]

In other words, only God can save the world from ultimate tragedy. But to the extent that God is Beauty, then yes, the world will be saved by beauty, which in this case is the beauty of an eternal being who is simultaneously Beautifier, Beauty, and Beautifulness.[11] This Beauty exists beyond the world but also entered the world as Jesus of Nazareth, who lived a beautiful life, died a horrific death, rose again, ascended to heaven, and sent the Spirit to bring a whole new creation to life. This is the sort of beauty that will save the world: trinitarian beauty, revealed beauty, incarnate beauty, cruciform beauty, resurrected beauty, ascended beauty, spirited beauty.[12] This beauty is foolishness to the world because it goes belonging to death as well as resurrected life.[13] As Chris Green states: "There can be no redemption without the death of Beauty in hell."[14] If this is true, then the world will be saved by dying and rising to new life with beauty.[15]

To die in the Beauty which dies is "to abandon oneself" into God's embrace, letting everything be transfigured in him who welcomes us into another, new Beauty.
—Bruno Forte, *The Portal of Beauty*[16]

What Sort of Beauty Will Save the World?

What sort of beauty will save the world? The two options considered so far are, in my opinion, compelling and complementary. The first option is that natural and artistic beauty can save us from apathy, aimlessness, and despair for as long as we are alive. Beauty makes this life breathable. The second option is that divine beauty revealed in Christ by the Spirit will save us from death and alienation from God. Beauty gives our souls oxygen for eternity. Unfortunately, those who believe beauty is oxygen for this life often dismiss the notion that beauty could be oxygen for eternal life, and vice versa. Could it be, however, that each view needs the other to describe the fullness of how beauty is oxygen for our souls both now and forever?

On the one hand, if it's true that natural and artistic beauty is oxygen because it makes this life breathable, by itself this view can turn encounters with beauty into a form of therapy, a self-help solution within a challenging life. There is no need for a beauty that disrupts every human attempt to figure things out and make life more manageable. On the other hand, if it's true that the beauty of the triune God is oxygen for eternal life, by itself this view can ignore or downplay the beauty of creation and human artistry. Like the old hymn goes, we "look full in his wonderful face, and the things of the earth will grow strangely dim in the light of his glory and grace."[17] If we're looking to "the things of the earth" to completely satisfy our souls, then this sentiment might be on target, but if keeping our eyes fixed on the beauty of Jesus diminishes the beauty of blue jays or Banksy's prophetic graffiti, then we're missing the full potential for God's beauty to be oxygen for our souls both now and forever.

Many churches, especially Protestant ones, have tried to banish earthly beauty from their worship spaces, deeming it a distraction from the beauty of a heavenly God (except the beauty of Scripture, of course, because it's divinely inspired). To do so, however, is to overlook all the ways God's beauty is present within such a space and how it incites our wonder and worship.

Sitting in church this past Sunday, I was joyfully overwhelmed by beauty: yes, the beauty of the gospel of the triune God, but also the beauty of the stained glass window, the smiles and greetings, the ringing of the bell, the old oak pews, the multicolored faces of the congregation, the strumming guitar and melodic piano, the swaying bodies and clapping hands, the confession and assurance, the prayers of the people, the impassioned preaching, the sharing of bread and wine. I don't want these beautiful, earthly things to fade away; they are oxygen for my soul. Whatever forms or aspects of worship you find alluring, you don't need to treat them as a distraction from the beauty of God.

Poet and professor Dana Gioia writes: "Whenever the Church has abandoned the notion of beauty, it has lost precisely the power that it hoped to cultivate—its ability to reach souls in the modern world. Is it any wonder that so many artists and intellectuals have fled the Church?"[18] Gioia is getting at something important, but in evaluating this predicament we must maintain an expansive notion of beauty, where beauty exists in ordinary, simple places and rituals as well as ornate, complex ones.

As the church (and others) seek to reclaim beauty, we need to embrace both the beauty of this world and the beauty of God, because if we abandon earthly beauty we are fleeing from the revelation and presence of God. Embracing earthly beauty is a way of encountering divine beauty and vice versa. The beauty that will save the world is not *either* the beauty of creation and artistry *or* the beauty of the triune God, but God's beauty revealed in Christ as well as through creation and human creativity. Only God through Christ by the Spirit can save the world in an ultimate sense, but God does so through ordinary and surprising means like the beautiful feet of those who bring good news.[19] And it's not only preachers who bring good news. The entire cosmos declares the glory of God, with humans adding to the display through the creative works of our hands.[20] This beauty is not separate from God's saving mission, but an integral part of how God entices, humbles, attracts, reveals, confronts, comforts, and unites all things in Christ by the Spirit.[21] Created beauty is also oxygen for our souls because the Spirit-Breath of God sustains, animates, and perfects created things.[22]

A lot of words have been written wrestling with the question of why a good God would create a world with so much suffering, but I am more interested in why God would create a world with so much beauty. Why all the diversity, grandeur, and intricate detail in nature? Why the astonishing design of the human body and mind? Why is it all so breathtaking? One answer is that the beauty of the world is an overflow of God's uncontainable beauty.[23] The world was created out of this abundance, and it will be sustained the same way.

The wonder is—given the errant nature of freedom and the burgeoning texture in time—the wonder is that all the forms are not monsters, that there is beauty at all, grace gratuitous, pennies found, like mockingbird's free fall. Beauty itself is the fruit of the creator's exuberance that grew such a tangle, and the grotesques and horrors bloom from that same free growth, that intricate scramble and twine up and down the conditions of time.

—Annie Dillard, *Pilgrim at Tinker Creek*[24]

If all that exists is already so extravagant, I can only imagine the glory yet to be revealed. We are already being saved by beauty, but one day beauty will save all of creation when it's "liberated from its bondage to decay and brought into the freedom and glory of the children of God."[25] Meanwhile, we groan, we wait, we hope, and we breathe in as much beauty as we can.[26] We participate in the Spirit's beautifying work. In a world in which "nonbeing sprawls" in the shape of ugliness and "people cease to believe that there is good and evil," it is beauty that "will call to them and save them."[27]

I like to imagine how beauty, like love, is as strong as death: unyielding, unquenchable, unstoppable.[28]

Sometimes when life and religion get cluttered and claustrophobic, you must cut away the accoutrements to breathe again.

The Reformational *solas* are an example of peeling back the layers to get back to the basics of how the world will be saved. *Sola fide*: faith alone; *sola gratia*: grace alone; *sola scriptura*: Scripture alone; *solus Christus*: Christ alone; *soli Deo gloria*: God's glory alone. These slogans were never intended to jettison everything else, like the importance of obedience, tradition, and a revelatory creation. Rather, they were a call to keep God's being and action at the center of the story, and they still have power to guide a church that always needs to be reformed. I wonder, however, if there are additional *solas* we need to shout from the rooftops today in an age of buffered, battered, and bored souls? *Sola forma*: beauty alone will save the world. *Solus spiritus Dei*: the Spirit-Breath of God alone is oxygen for our souls.

When we articulate what sort of beauty will save the world, the answer should be specific or else it easily becomes vacuous. As such, I appreciate the directness of Patitsas when he writes: "The *actual* Beauty that will save the world will be nothing less than the ultimate revelation of Christ and of him crucified. Such Beauty will save us because it will wipe away any trace of estrangement we have acquired towards God through the trauma in our lives."[29] This Beauty will save the world by making everything new.[30]

The salvation that will be revealed in the future is already available now as God's beauty whispers and roars through this world in both ordinary and surprising ways. This is the beauty that entices us to believe and to move beyond the suffocating boundaries of a buffered existence into a life of faith, grace, and joy. This is the beauty that brings hope and healing despite all the troubles and the trauma we carry. This is the beauty that stirs up wonder within our ordinary and monotonous lives, compelling us to risk more love and creativity. Beauty is oxygen, and there is more than enough to go around.

Questions and Practices

Chapter One: Learning to Breathe

Did you remember to take deep breaths as you read through
this chapter?

What are the similarities between oxygen for your body and
beauty for your soul?

What associations do you have with the word *soul*? Are there
some that need to be challenged and others you need to
cultivate?

Are you tempted to treat beauty as less necessary than truth or
goodness? How might that impact your life?

How has beauty been oxygen for your soul even during this
ordinary day?

Learn the benefit of deep breathing and practice this each time
you see the solitary "O" on the page.

Begin a beauty journal in which you jot down at least one encounter with beauty every day. If you have a daily prayer
practice, fold this into your gratitude and praise.

Share about a place in nature you find beautiful and helps you breathe. If you have a photo or can take one, share it with a friend or on social media using the hashtag #beautyisoxygen.

Chapter Two: A Suffocating Life

Do you have a habit of saying you're fine even when you're not?

How does the feeling of meh show up in your life and what do you do to deal with it?

Where does your life feel least breathable?

How might the problem be worse than you think and the good news far better than you imagined?

In your beauty journal, add to the list of things mentioned by Sam Wells (p. 36) that were never really yours after all.

Repent of whatever is preventing you from encountering beauty, perhaps making O'Connor's prayer your own.

Think about or discuss the similarities between the moon and your experience of beauty: its many phases, its illumination from another source, the reasons for an eclipse.

Chapter Three: The Breeze of Beauty

What makes you say *wow!* instead of *meh*?

When have you been overcome by beauty, and did you find that experience delightful, threatening, or both?

How often do you allow yourself to pay sustained attention to beauty?

Have you ever considered how the whole story of God is about beauty and how that might change the way you relate to God?

How might the beauty of art widen the circumference of your neighborly love?

Take a walk in the woods and try out the practice of silent forest bathing with all your senses attuned to the breeze of beauty. What do you see, smell, hear, touch, think, feel, and imagine? Take a picture to remember the experience. #beautyisoxygen.

Identify a night when the moon is dim to enjoy some stargazing, getting away from city lights the best you can. Record the experience in your beauty journal.

Lose yourself in a good novel and perhaps invite a friend to do the same so you can talk about the story and how its beauty impacts you.

Chapter Four: Asphyxiations of Counterfeit Beauty

How have you been tempted to embrace counterfeit beauty?

Have you ever been battered by abusive beauty standards that made it difficult to embrace the fact that you are fearfully and wonderfully made?

What can you do to welcome beauty that has bite, grit, and maybe even a side of terror?

Have you been conditioned to think of beauty as wasteful or unnecessary?

Are there are places in life where you need to let the beautiful edges go wild?

Visit an art museum and see if you can spot any expressions of counterfeit beauty, particularly one that celebrates white skin tones over colorful ones. Write about the experience in your beauty journal.

Find an expression of beauty in nature or a social situation where several colors, textures, and shapes collide. Take a photo, share it with a friend, or post it with the hashtag #beautyisoxygen and a description of why all the combinations and differences are beautiful.

Permit yourself to lament environmental destruction, perhaps by listening to *Climate Vigil Songs* by Porter's Gate. Then commit to specific ways of preserving or enhancing the beauty of creation—maybe starting a small garden, planting a tree, or spreading some wildflower seeds.

Chapter Five: Healing Breaths of Fresh Beauty

How might beauty be inviting you into greater delight and pleasure?

Is the beauty of the world leading you away from or more deeply into communion with God?

What beautiful things are drawing you into healthy attachments?

When is the last time you've read, listened to, or watched a good fairy tale?

How has or could beauty minister to you in your pain?

Write about a place, person, object, or artwork that gives you hope, and what this hope has to do with beauty.

Think of a situation or problem in your life and start asking "what if?" questions as a way of imagining various paths forward and abundant solutions. Ask someone to dream alongside you.

Create your own Ebenezer collage by collecting some daily items that evoke perseverance, joy, and hope, and gluing them together on a board or canvas. Take a photo of your collage and post it using #beautyisoxygen.

Chapter Six: Boredom and the Ache for Beauty

Have you ever experienced stifling boredom? What, if anything, has alleviated it?

Have you ever experienced generative boredom as a springboard for fresh creativity?

Do you believe that beauty comes to those who wait? Why or why not?

Is there a monotonous routine in your life you could reimagine and reengage as a soul stirring activity?

What, if anything, is keeping you from embracing slowness and making beauty your objective?

Try Capon's exercise of slicing an onion, and don't take any shortcuts.

Pay attention to another familiar item or living being and make an entry in your beauty journal about anything new you notice or any reason to be astonished. If it's fitting, post about it using #beautyisoxygen.

The next time you find yourself waiting, whether in line or at a stoplight or in a gate area at the airport, embrace it as an opportunity to look for beauty without taking out your phone or choosing another way to pass the time.

Chapter Seven: The Beautiful Ordinary

Do you view ordinary times and places as bereft of beauty?

How might recognizing God's presence, action, and beauty within the mundane shift your attitude and perspective?

What makes it most challenging for you to be fully present wherever you are?

When did you last pause to contemplate the clouds?

Choose a day to practice a breath prayer at each major transition, like getting up, switching tasks, going into a meeting, getting into the car, arriving back home. Inhale: *Attune my senses* . . . Exhale: *To the beauty of this moment.*

Gather some people together to watch a movie set in another world. Afterwards, talk about what moved you and how it might help you reimagine your own story.

Whether or not it's your regular practice, observe an entire Sabbath day in which you set work aside to rest, pay attention, and delight in beauty. If corporate worship is a part of your rhythm, start there, and then let wonder be your guide for the rest of the day.

Reflect and talk to someone else about how you express creativity, whether at work, at home, or with a hobby.

Chapter Eight: What Sort of Beauty Will Save the World?

Have you ever felt like your life was being saved by beauty?

Do you believe that beauty will save the world? If so, what sort of beauty might that be?

Are you ever tempted to choose between the beauty of God and the beauty of the world?

How might the reality of a beautiful world help you generate new questions?

Are you ready and willing to breathe in beauty as oxygen for your soul?

Write in your beauty journal about other ways beauty is strong.

Commit to several practical ways to breathe in beauty daily.

Bask in the beauty of God and let it fill your lungs for life.

Acknowledgments

The phrase *beauty is oxygen* originated during a 2017 Lenten sermon series called Soul Pollution at Warehouse 242 in Charlotte, North Carolina. The purpose of this series was to highlight ways our souls can suffer by leaving unquestioned certain normalized assumptions and patterns in our life, things like achievement, sentimentality, comparison, security, indifference, and authenticity. Are the things we normalize polluting our lives? When we acknowledge those things, how can beauty be oxygen for our souls and motivate us to embrace a different way of life?

I have deep appreciation for Steve Whitby, then creative director at Warehouse 242, who always suggested ways to make a sermon series relatable, actionable, and imaginative. For this series, he proposed having a prompt for each day of Lent, sending it out on social media, and encouraging people to reflect on the prompt using field guides and to post about their experiences using the hashtag #beautyisoxygen. I'm delighted to bring that hashtag back to life and to introduce the idea of a "beauty journal" in the Questions and Practices section. I also want to acknowledge Mike Lawrie and Holly Norton, each of whom preached one week during the Soul Pollution series and engaged with the topic of beauty in generative ways.

I continued to explore the notion that beauty is oxygen in fall 2021 when I taught a Wednesday evening class with the title "Beauty Is Oxygen: How the Arts Can Help Our Souls Breathe" at First Presbyterian Church in Tulsa. I am deeply grateful to lead pastor Dr. Jim Miller for giving me free rein to teach this course during my time as Theologian in Residence, and for all the folks who showed up, engaged, and offered thoughtful responses, especially Joel and Sarah Donohue and Mark Brown. The beautiful environment and people of First Church Tulsa were oxygen for my soul in so many ways, and I thank God for such a beautiful church.

As the book indicates, many places, people, creatures, and works of art have shaped my own journey with beauty, and one of the most notable places is Stonewood Acres in central Minnesota, the 160-acre homestead where I lived during junior and senior high school and returned many times in subsequent years. I've dedicated this book to Stonewood Acres as the place where beauty tuned my heart to sing God's grace.

My family is the primary relational context for breathing in beauty, and I'm constantly amazed by the gift of Stephanie and our three children: Eden, Beata, and Chalmer. They help me keep the wonder alive and have cheered me on in this attempt to capture some of it in words.

I'm grateful to Gordon-Conwell Theological Seminary and a vocation that encourages and gives space for writing and reflection. I want to thank Dr. Gerry Wheaton in particular for embracing a vision for integrating theology and the arts and making a way for me to have a place at the table.

Acknowledgments

At a time when my perseverance in writing was waning, Lisa Ann Cockrel at Eerdmans saw the potential for this book and gave needed encouragement for me to keep going. My deep appreciation also extends to copyeditor Christopher Reese and to Jenny Hoffman and the whole team at Eerdmans.

I am indebted to Melanee Marshall, Dave Reinhardt, Ben Sammons, and Stephanie Vander Lugt for attentive, kind, and wise feedback on the manuscript, all of which refined this book into something much more readable.

Finally, thank you reader for your interest in this book and an openness to how beauty is oxygen for your soul. If anything in these pages resonates and leads you into a more breathable life, my joy in crafting these words would be complete. As Annie Dillard observes: "Why are we reading, if not in the hope of beauty laid bare, life heightened, and its deepest mystery probed?"[1]

Notes

FOREWORD

1. Haruki Murakami, *Novelist as a Vocation* (New York: Alfred Knopf, 2015), 13.

INTRODUCTION

1. G. K. Chesterton, *Orthodoxy* (1908; repr., New York: Doubleday, 2001), 23.

2. A book that helpfully addresses the history of philosophical abuses is Arthur Danto, *The Abuse of Beauty: Aesthetics and the Concept of Art* (Chicago: Open Court, 2003).

3. Roger Scruton traces other reasons for what he calls "the flight from beauty" in *Beauty: A Very Short Introduction* (Oxford: Oxford University Press, 2011), 139–61.

4. William Desmond, *The Gift of Beauty and the Passion of Being: On the Threshold between the Aesthetic and the Religious* (Eugene: Cascade, 2018), 108.

5. Annie Dillard, *Pilgrim at Tinker Creek* (1974; repr., New York: Harper Perennial, 1998), 9.

6. See Karl Barth, *Church Dogmatics*, vol. II/1, ed. Geoffrey W. Bromiley and T. F. Torrance, trans. Geoffrey W. Bromiley et al. (Edinburgh: T&T Clark, 1957), 653.

7. For example, Thomas Aquinas identified three conditions of beauty: "integrity or perfection, since those things which are impaired are by the very fact ugly; due proportion or harmony; and lastly, brightness or clarity, whence things are called beautiful which have a bright color." Thomas Aquinas, *The Summa Theologica*, trans. the Fathers of the English Dominican Province, 2nd rev. ed. (1920), I, q. 39, art. 8.

8. Dillard, *Pilgrim at Tinker Creek*, 10.

9. Charles Taylor, *A Secular Age* (Cambridge: Belknap Press, 2007), 542-57.

10. Calvin Seerveld, *Rainbows for a Fallen World* (Toronto: Toronto Tuppence Press, 1980), 121.

11. James K. A. Smith, "Besides, Before, Beyond Beauty," in *Image*, issue 102.

12. This line is taken from Christian Wiman's poem "Every Riven Thing," found in a stunning collection of poems that also bears this title. Christian Wiman, *Every Riven Thing* (New York: Farrar, Straus and Giroux, 2011), 24-25.

13. The "sublime" has a long history in philosophy and the arts, and generally means a quality of grandeur or transcendence with no specific reference to the reality of a triune God. For an overview of the concept, see Timothy M. Costelloe, *The Sublime: From Antiquity to the Present* (Cambridge: Cambridge University Press, 2012).

14. Wiman, "Every Riven Thing."

15. Hebrews 1:3.

16. See Bruce Herman, "Wounds and Beauty," in *The Beauty of God: Theology and the Arts*, ed. Daniel J. Treier, Mark Husbands, and Roger Lundin (Downers Grove: InterVarsity Press, 2007), 110-21.

17. Chesterton, *Orthodoxy*, 23.

CHAPTER I

1. Gerard Manley Hopkins, "The Blessed Virgin Compared to the Air We Breathe," in *Poems and Prose* (New York: Penguin, 1953), 54.

2. Mary Oliver, "Oxygen," in *New and Selected Poems: Volume Two* (Boston: Beacon Press, 2005), 25.

3. For more information on the benefits of deep breathing, see James Nestor, *Breath: The New Science of a Lost Art* (New York: Riverhead Books, 2021).

4. Duncan MacDougall originally proposed this theory in a scientific study published in 1907. This myth continues to appear throughout popular culture, like in the 2003 film *21 Grams* or a popular episode of *Ted Lasso* ("No Weddings and a Funeral," September 24, 2021).

5. Cf. Genesis 1:20, 24; 2:7; Leviticus 17:11, 14.

6. English Standard Version.

7. *Soul*, written by Pete Docter, Mike Jones, and Kemp Powers, directed by Pete Docter (Walt Disney Pictures and Pixar Animation Studios, 2020).

8. Terry Tempest Williams, *Erosion* (New York: Sarah Crichton Books, 2019), 17.

9. Hopkins, "The Blessed Virgin Compared to the Air We Breathe."

10. Wiman, "Every Riven Thing."

11. Rita Dove, "Scarf," in *Playlist for the Apocalypse: Poems* (New York: W. W. Norton, 2021), 12.

12. David Bentley Hart, *The Beauty of the Infinite: The Aesthetics of Christian Truth* (Grand Rapids: Eerdmans, 2013), 16.

13. Ross Gay, *The Book of Delights* (Chapel Hill: Workmans' Publishing, 2019), 138–40.

14. Gay, *The Book of Delights*, 221.

15. Bahar Orang, *Where Things Touch: A Meditation on Beauty* (Toronto: Book*hug Press, 2020), 29.

16. Ralph Waldo Emerson, *Nature and Selected Essays* (New York: Penguin, 2003), 44.

17. Fyodor Dostoevsky, *The Brothers Karamazov*, trans. Constance Garnett (New York: Modern Library, 1996), 117.

18. Wendy Farley, *Beguiled by Beauty: Cultivating a Life of Contemplation and Compassion* (Louisville: Westminster John Knox, 2020), 43.

19. D. H. Lawrence, "Nottingham and the Mining Country," *The New Adelphi* 3, no. 4 (June-August 1930). He made this observation to explain why a coal miner would buy a piano.

20. Brian Doyle, "What Do Poems *Do*?" in *How the Light Gets In and Other Headlong Epiphanies* (Maryknoll, NY: Orbis, 2015), 8.

21. William Carlos Williams, "Asphodel, That Greeny Flower," in *Asphodel, That Greeny Flower & Other Love Poems* (New York: New Directions Books, 1994), 19.

22. For a summary of recent debates, see Ferris Jabr, "How Beauty Is Making Scientists Rethink Evolution," in *New York Times Magazine*, January 9, 2019. The article concludes: "If there is a universal truth about beauty—some concise and elegant concept that encompasses every variety of charm and grace in existence—we do not yet understand enough about nature to articulate it."

23. Hans Rookmaaker, *Art Needs No Justification* (1978; repr., Vancouver: Regent College Publishing, 2010).

24. Exodus 28:33–34.

25. Natalie Carnes, *Beauty: A Theological Engagement with Gregory of Nyssa* (Eugene: Cascade, 2014), 57.

26. Dietrich von Hildebrand, *Aesthetics*, vol. 1, trans. Hildebrand Project (Steubenville, OH: Hildebrand Project, 2016), 305.

27. Robert Farrar Capon, *The Supper of the Lamb: A Culinary Reflection* (New York: Modern Library, 2002), 85–86.

28. Exodus 33.

29. Philippians 2:12–13.

30. C. S. Lewis, *The Lion, the Witch and the Wardrobe* (New York: HarperCollins, 1950), 86.

31. Hopkins, "God's Grandeur," in *Poems and Prose*, 27.

CHAPTER 2

1. Charles Taylor introduced us to the notion of the premodern "porous self," which gave way to the "buffered self" of modernity as it came to fruition in the West. Taylor, *A Secular Age*.

2. Here I am commenting on the culture of the premodern West, acknowledging that other cultures have less dualistic cosmologies and did not experience the shift from porous to buffered souls in the same way.

3. Taylor, *A Secular Age*, 38.

4. *Friends*, Season 10, Episode 2, "The One Where Ross Is Fine," October 2, 2003.

5. Aerosmith put crass but honest words to this in their 1989 song "F.I.N.E."

6. Taylor, *A Secular Age*, 309.

7. Andrew Root, *The Pastor in a Secular Age: Ministry to People Who No Longer Need a God* (Grand Rapids: Baker Academic, 2019), 66–67.

8. *The Simpsons*, Season 12, Episode 15, "Hungry, Hungry Homer," March 4, 2001.

9. "A Portrait of the Decade," BBC News online, December 14, 2009, http://news.bbc.co.uk/2/hi/uk_news/magazine/8406898.stm.

10. Samantha Henig, "The Meh List: Not Hot, Not Not, Just

Meh," September 28, 2014, https://www.nytimes.com/interactive/2014/09/28/magazine/28-one-page-magazine.html.

11. Taylor, *A Secular Age*, 539.

12. G-Eazy and Bebe Rexha, "Me, Myself, and I," track 3 on *When It's Dark Out* (RCA, 2015).

13. Taylor, *A Secular Age*, 594.

14. Julian Barnes, *Nothing to Be Frightened Of* (New York: Alfred Knopf, 2008), 1.

15. Desmond, *The Gift of Beauty and the Passion of Being*, 125–27.

16. *American Beauty*, written by Alan Ball, directed by Sam Mendes (DreamWorks Pictures, 1999).

17. Galatians 3:10.

18. Martin Luther, *Luther's Works*, ed. Hilton C. Oswald, vol. 25, *Lectures on Romans* (Saint Louis: Concordia, 1972), 291.

19. Galatians 3:13–14.

20. February 23/March 2, 2015.

21. I'm grateful to Dave Reinhardt for bringing this insight to my attention.

22. Hans Urs von Balthasar, *The Glory of the Lord: A Theological Aesthetics*, trans. Erasmo Leiva-Merikakis, vol. 1, *Seeing the Form* (Edinburgh: T&T Clark, 1992), 18.

23. Ezekiel 36:26.

24. Søren Kierkegaard, *The Sickness unto Death: A Christian Psychological Exposition of Education and Awakening by Anti-Climacus* (New York: Penguin Classics, 1989).

25. Sam Wells, *Walk Humbly: Encouragements for Living, Working, and Being* (Grand Rapids: Eerdmans, 2019), 21–22.

26. Paraphrasing Revelation 3:18–20.

27. Flannery O'Connor, *A Prayer Journal* (New York: Farrar, Straus and Giroux, 2013), 3. Given new research emerging about O'Connor and race, perhaps her "self-shadow" includes a troubling double-mindedness and "radical ambivalence" about race and civil

rights. See Angela Alaimo O'Donnell, *Radical Ambivalence: Race in Flannery O'Connor* (New York: Fordham University Press, 2020).

28. As Annie Dillard writes: "beauty is something objectively performed—the tree that falls in the forest—having being externally, stumbled across or missed, as real and present as both sides of the moon." Dillard, *Pilgrim at Tinker Creek*, 107–8.

CHAPTER 3

1. M. Amos Clifford, *Your Guide to Forest Bathing: Experience the Healing Power of Nature* (Red Wheel, 2021), 4.

2. Genesis 1:2; cf. Psalm 33:6. The Hebrew word *ruach* is usually translated here as *Spirit* but literally means *wind* or *breath*.

3. Revelation 22:2.

4. Beck, "Wow," track 7 on *Colors* (Capital Records, 2017).

5. Post Malone, "Wow," track 17 on *Hollywood's Bleeding* (Republic Records, 2019).

6. Kate Bush, "Wow," track 3 on *Lionheart* (EMI Records, 1978).

7. Zara Larsson, "Wow," track 5 on *Poster Girl* (Epic Records, 2021).

8. Luke 19:40.

9. Bill Manhire, "Wow," in *Wow* (Manchester: Carcanet Press, 2020), 55.

10. Elaine Scarry, *On Beauty and Being Just* (Princeton: Princeton University Press, 1999), 111–12.

11. Abigail Carroll, "Creed," in *Habitation of Wonder* (Eugene: Cascade, 2018), 115.

12. Ross Gay, "Babies. Seriously," in *The Book of Delights*, 153.

13. John O'Donohue, *Beauty: The Invisible Embrace* (New York: HarperCollins, 2004), 20.

14. Farley, *Beguiled by Beauty*, 42, 50.

15. Rebecca Solnit notes how American publications like *Walking* are little more than fitness magazines, whereas in the UK there

are many magazines "in which walking is about the beauty of the landscape rather than the body," showing how walking can extend an egocentric lifestyle or foster a decentering one. The point is not that fitness is inherently egocentric, but that walking is not automatically a beauty-attentive, unselfing activity. Rebecca Solnit, *Wanderlust: A History of Walking* (New York: Penguin, 2001), 173.

16. C. S. Lewis, *An Experiment in Criticism* (1961; repr., Cambridge: Cambridge University Press, 2012), 138, 141.

17. Dietrich von Hildebrand, *Beauty in the Light of Redemption* (Steubenville, OH: Hildebrand Press, 2019), 63, 65.

18. Frederick Buechner, *The Remarkable Ordinary* (Grand Rapids: Zondervan, 2017), 22–23.

19. Buechner, *The Remarkable Ordinary*, 21–22.

20. Matthew B. Crawford, *The World Beyond Your Head: On Becoming an Individual in an Age of Distraction* (New York: Farrar, Straus and Giroux, 2016).

21. For more on disponibility as the core of Christian formation, see Wesley Vander Lugt, *Living Theodrama: Reimagining Theological Ethics* (London: Routledge, 2014), 33–47.

22. Hildebrand, *Aesthetics*, 1:373.

23. Rowan Williams, *The Wound of Knowledge*, 2nd ed. (Lanham, MD: Cowley Publications, 1991), 188. In a similar vein, Clyde Kilby contends that "great art enables one to transcend the shoddy and dictatorial self which has possession of most of us much of the time by dismissing or escaping this self through 'living into' the symbolized presentation of reality in that art." Clyde Kilby, *The Arts and Christian Imagination: Essays on Art, Literature, and Aesthetics* (Brewster, MA: Paraclete Press, 2016), 22.

24. Taylor, *A Secular Age*, 730.

25. Luke 12:27.

26. Calvin Seerveld uses the word "bewonderment" to talk about this practice. Calvin Seerveld, *Bewondering God's Dumb-*

founding Doings: God Talking to Us Little People in the Final Book of the Bible (Jordan Station, Ontario, Canada: Paideia Press, 2020).

27. Emerson, *Nature and Selected Essays*, 37.

28. Taylor, *A Secular Age*, 360.

29. Taylor, *A Secular Age*, 595–617.

30. Taylor, *A Secular Age*, 518.

31. The early church theologian Pseudo-Dionysius the Areopagite was the first to overtly identify beauty as one of the divine names. Pseudo-Dionysius the Areopagite, *The Divine Names; The Mystical Theology*, trans. John D. Jones (Milwaukee: Marquette University Press, 1980). Contemporary theologian Brendan Thomas Sammon revives this divine-name approach to a theology of beauty in *Called to Attraction: An Introduction to the Theology of Beauty* (Eugene: Cascade, 2017).

32. The same is true about transcendence in nature, but Begbie limits his argument to transcendence in the arts.

33. Jeremy Begbie, *Redeeming Transcendence in the Arts: Bearing Witness to the Triune God* (Grand Rapids: Eerdmans, 2018), 166–67.

34. Orang, *Where Things Touch*, 42.

35. Ephesians 4:6.

36. Carnes, *Beauty*, 108; 121.

37. Romans 1:20–21.

38. Mark 8:18.

39. Begbie, *Redeeming Transcendence in the Arts*, 123.

40. Riffing off John 1:1–4; cf. Acts 17:25.

41. Genesis 2:7.

42. After Gerard Manley Hopkins who stated: "Christ plays in ten thousand places, lovely in limbs and lovely in eyes not his." Hopkins, "As Kingfishers Catch Fire," in *Poems and Prose*, 51.

43. John 1:14.

44. Ezekiel 37:4–6.

45. Ezekiel 36:26; Ephesians 2:1.

46. John 20:22.

47. Karl Barth, *Church Dogmatics*, vol. II/1, ed. Geoffrey W. Bromiley and T. F. Torrance, trans. Geoffrey W. Bromiley et al. (Edinburgh: T&T Clark, 1957), 661.

48. Martin Schleske, *The Sound of Life's Unspeakable Beauty*, trans. Janet Leigh Gesme (Grand Rapids: Eerdmans, 2020), 135.

49. See Norman Wirzba, *This Sacred Life: Humanity's Place in a Wounded World* (Cambridge: Cambridge University Press, 2021). 87.

50. John 15:1–8.

51. Makoto Fujimura, *Art and Faith: A Theology of Making* (New Haven: Yale University Press, 2020), 85.

52. For a recent study, see Mary W. McCampbell, *Imagining Our Neighbors as Ourselves: How Art Shapes Empathy* (Minneapolis: Fortress Press, 2022). See also Stephanie Curry, "Art and Empathy: Four Thought Leaders Explain the Connection," Minneapolis Institute of Art, May 7, 2021, https://new.artsmia.org/stories/art-and-empathy-four-thought-leaders-explain-the-connection.

53. For the power of the novel in this regard, see Nicholas Wolterstorff, *Art Rethought: The Social Practices of Art* (Oxford: Oxford University Press, 2015), 215.

54. Alan Paton, *Cry, the Beloved Country* (London: Jonathan Cape, 1949).

55. Keillor in *Lake Wobegon Days* (New York: Viking, 1985) did for me what Dostoevsky in *The Brothers Karamazov* did for Eugene Peterson: "He trained my antennae to pick up the suppressed signals of spirituality in the denatured stock language of these conversations, discovering tragic plots and comic episodes, works-in-progress all around me . . . there were no ordinary people . . . there was drama enough in this vanishing cornfield to carry me for a lifetime." Eugene Peterson, *Under the Unpredictable Plant: An Exploration in Vocational Holiness* (Grand Rapids: Eerdmans, 1992), 62–63.

56. *Thin Red Line*, written and directed by Terrence Malick (20th Century Fox, 1998).

57. Jonathan Larson, *Rent* (premiered at the New York Theatre Workshop, January 25, 1996).

58. Alan Noble, *Disruptive Witness: Speaking Truth in a Distracted Age* (Downers Grove: InterVarsity Press, 2018). See also Alan Noble, "The Disruptive Witness of Art," in *Our Secular Age: Ten Years of Reading and Applying Charles Taylor*, ed. Collin Hansen (Deerfield, IL: The Gospel Coalition, 2017), 135–45.

59. Kehinde Wiley, *Philip the Fair*, 2006, oil and enamel on canvas, 112 × 86″, Mint Museum, Charlotte, North Carolina.

60. Timothy G. Patitsas, *The Ethics of Beauty* (Maysville, MO: St Nicholas Press, 2020), 76. Ultimately, we don't leave ourselves behind in the depth of love, but we lose ourselves only to receive a new self.

61. Graham Greene, *The Power and the Glory*, 50th anniversary ed. (New York: Penguin, 2015), 133.

62. McCampbell, *Imagining Our Neighbors as Ourselves*.

63. Ephesians 2:8–10.

64. Begbie, *Redeeming Transcendence in the Arts*, 167.

65. C. S. Lewis, "The Weight of Glory," in *The Weight of Glory and Other Addresses* (New York: HarperOne, 2001), 30.

66. Lewis, "The Weight of Glory," 41.

67. Many versions exist of "St. Patrick's Breastplate," and this version is slightly adapted from the traditional prayer rather than the hymn adaptation by Cecil Alexander and Charles Stanford.

CHAPTER 4

1. "The ethical must belong, for theology, to an aesthetics of desire: of gratuity, grace, pleasure, eros, and interest at once." Hart, *Beauty of the Infinite*, 265. See also Stanley Hauerwas, *Vision and*

Virtue: Essays in Christian Ethical Reflection (Notre Dame: University of Notre Dame Press, 1981).

2. Willie James Jennings traces the history and theory of this in *The Christian Imagination: Theology and the Origins of Race* (New Haven: Yale University Press, 2010).

3. Sally Rooney, *Beautiful World, Where Are You?* (New York: Farrar, Straus, and Giroux, 2021), 83.

4. Mike Bakers, Jennifer Valentino-DeVries, Manny Fernandez, and Michael La Forgia, "Three Words. 70 Cases. The Tragic History of 'I Can't Breathe,'" *New York Times*, June 29, 2020, https://www.nytimes.com/interactive/2020/06/28/us/i-cant-breathe-police-arrest.html.

5. Meera Senthilingam, Pallabi Munsi, and Vanessa Offiong, "Skin Whitening: What Is It, What Are the Risks and Who Profits?" *CNN*, January 25, 2022, https://edition.cnn.com/2022/01/25/world/as-equals-skin-whitening-global-market-explainer-intl-cmd/index.html.

6. The word "colorism" is often traced back to Alice Walker's *In Search of Our Mother's Gardens: Womanist Prose* (San Diego: Harcourt Brace Jovanovich, 1983).

7. Lyrics from Katherine Lee Bates, "America the Beautiful," 1893.

8. Jennings, *The Christian Imagination*, 58–59.

9. Jennings, *The Christian Imagination*, 292. At the end of his book, Jennings describes the power of a new Christian social imagination that requires imagining social connection and mystical joining in a whole new way.

10. Revelation 7:9.

11. David Bentley Hart traces the theological and aesthetic value of difference in relation to "the superabounding joy, delight, regard, and response that is God's life" and the world he created. Hart, *The Beauty of the Infinite*, 183.

12. Hart, *The Beauty of the Infinite*, 258.

13. Hopkins, "Pied Beauty," in *Poems and Prose*, 30.

14. Ta-Nehisi Coates, "Hope and the Artist: The Virtues of Enlightenment over Feel-Goodism," *The Atlantic*, November 23, 2015.

15. Ta-Nehisi Coates, *Between the World and Me* (New York: Spiegel and Grau, 2015), 10.

16. C. S. Lewis, *The Collected Letters of C. S. Lewis*, vol. 1, ed. Walter Hooper (San Francisco: HarperCollins, 2004), 176. Lewis explains: "a word I've coined to mean terror and beauty."

17. Makoto Fujimura, *Silence and Beauty: Hidden Faith Born of Suffering* (Downers Grove: InterVarsity Press, 2016), 65.

18. Fujimura, *Silence and Beauty*, 102.

19. Jeremy Begbie, "Beauty, Sentimentality, and the Arts," in *A Peculiar Orthodoxy: Reflections on Theology and the Arts* (Grand Rapids: Baker Academic, 2018), 25–48.

20. Thomas Kinkade as quoted in Gregory Wolfe, "Editorial Statement: The Painter of Lite," *Image* 34 (2002): 5.

21. Calvin Seerveld, *A Christian Critique of Art and Literature* (Sioux Center: Dordt College Press, 1995), 49–50.

22. Psalm 50:2–3.

23. Mary Oliver, *Upstream: Selected Essays* (New York: Penguin, 2019), 113.

24. Christian Wiman, *My Bright Abyss: Meditation of a Modern Believer* (New York: Farrar, Straus and Giroux, 2013), 3.

25. Karl Barth, *Church Dogmatics*, II/2, 665.

26. Steven R. Guthrie, *Creator Spirit: The Holy Spirit and the Art of Becoming Human* (Grand Rapids: Baker, 2011), 199.

27. Wiman, *My Bright Abyss*, 19.

28. Isaiah 53:2b.

29. Isaiah 53:3–5.

30. Jason Farago, "The Role of Art in a Time of War," *New York*

Times, July 28, 2022, https://www.nytimes.com/2022/07/28/arts/design/ukraine-war-art-culture.html.

31. Matthew 26:6–9.

32. Matthew 26:10.

33. The common term for this age is the "Anthropocene." For a good discussion of the dynamics of life within the Anthropocene, see Wirzba, *This Sacred Life*, 3–33.

34. Pope Francis, "*Laudato si'*: Care for Our Common Home," May 24, 2015, https://www.vatican.va/content/francesco/en/encyclicals/documents/papa-francesco_20150524_enciclica-laudato-si.html, 26.

35. Sara Schumacher, "The Artist and the Environmental Crisis," in *The Art of New Creation: Trajectories in Theology and the Arts*, ed. Jeremy Begbie, Daniel Train, W. David O. Taylor (Downers Grove: IVP Academic, 2022), 100.

36. Bayo Akomolafe, *These Wilds Beyond Our Fences: Letters to My Daughter on Humanity's Search for Home* (Berkeley: North Atlantic Books, 2017).

37. Abigail Carroll, "How to Prepare for the Second Coming," in *Habitation of Wonder* (Eugene: Cascade, 2018), 106.

CHAPTER 5

1. C. S. Lewis, "Learning in War-Time," in *The Weight of Glory and Other Addresses*, 50. In citing this essay, I am not necessarily endorsing Lewis's views on war or heaven and hell, but I am aligning with his insistence that art and beauty are essential in times of crisis.

2. Lewis, "Learning in War-Time," 51.

3. Isak Dinesen, *Babette's Feast* (Victoria, BC: Reading Essentials, 1958). Most familiar is the film adaptation *Babette's Feast*, written and directed by Gabriel Axel (Nordisk Film, 1987).

4. *Joyeux Noël*, written and directed by Christian Carion (Nord-Ouest Films, 2005).

5. You can view photos of this ongoing *Mural of Brotherhood* at www.instagram.com/muraldelahermandad/.

6. Eugene H. Peterson, *The Message* (Colorado Springs: Nav-Press, 2002).

7. John Piper, *Desiring God: Meditations of a Christian Hedonist*, rev. ed. (Colorado Springs: Multnomah, 2011), 293.

8. See Peterson's paraphrase of Ecclesiastes 9 above. For a brief reflection on the need to delight in colors and scarves, especially as someone who might have inherited some dangerous assumptions, see Ross Gay, *The Book of Delights*, 91–93.

9. Ecclesiastes 12:1.

10. Saint Augustine, *Confessions*, trans. Henry Chadwick (Oxford: Oxford University Press, 1991), 201.

11. Augustine, *Confessions*, 210.

12. Augustine, *Confessions*, 210.

13. Edvard Munch, *The Scream,* 1893, oil, tempera, pastel, and crayon on cardboard, 36 x 28.9 ", National Museum, Oslo, Norway, https://www.nasjonalmuseet.no/en/collection/object/NG.M.00 939.

14. Samuel Beckett, *Waiting for Godot: A Tragicomedy in Two Acts* (1954; repr., New York: Grove Press, 2011).

15. Kendrick Lamar, "United in Grief," track 1 on *Mr. Morale & the Big Steppers* (Top Dawg Entertainment, 2022).

16. Emily Dickinson, "Tell All the Truth but Tell It Slant," in *The Complete Poems of Emily Dickinson*, ed. Thomas H. Johnson (New York: Back Bay Books, 1976), 506–7.

17. Jeremy Begbie, *Resounding Truth: Christian Wisdom in a World of Music* (Grand Rapids: Baker Academic, 2007), 302.

18. As a reminder, the soul includes the entirety of who we are,

including our bodies and minds. For more on the nature of trauma, see Bessel A. van der Kolk, *The Body Keeps Score: Brain, Mind, and Body in the Healing of Trauma* (New York: Penguin, 2015).

19. Patitsas, *The Ethics of Beauty*, 90.

20. Patitsas, *The Ethics of Beauty*, 79.

21. Abigail Carroll, "What Men Die For Lack Of," in *Habitation of Wonder*, 80. Carroll's poem pieces together lines from other famous poems, thus extending the insight of William Carlos Williams that "it is difficult to get the news from poems, yet men die miserably every day for lack of what is found there."

22. David Bentley Hart, *The Experience of God: Being, Consciousness, Bliss* (New York: Yale University Press, 2013), 280.

23. Kathryn B. Alexander, *Saving Beauty: A Theological Aesthetics of Nature* (Minneapolis: Fortress Press, 2014), 146.

24. 1 Corinthians 15:58.

25. See his argument in Coates, "Hope and the Artist."

26. Farley, *Beguiled by Beauty*, 49.

27. John W. de Gruchy, *Christianity, Art, and Transformation: Theological Aesthetics in the Struggle for Justice* (Cambridge: Cambridge University Press, 2001), 212.

28. Sarah Clarkson, *This Beautiful Truth: How God's Goodness Breaks into Our Darkness* (Grand Rapids: Baker, 2021), 30.

29. Cole Arthur Riley, *This Here Flesh: Spirituality, Liberation, and the Stories that Make Us* (New York: Convergent Books, 2022), 29.

30. Although the popular TV show *Floor Is Lava* evidently shows that adults love imaginative play as well, especially when it's combined with competition and risk.

31. *The Stinky & Dirty Show*, created by Guy Toubes (Amazon Studios and Brown Bag Films, January 15, 2015–August 23, 2019).

32. Shel Silverstein, "Whatif," in *A Light in the Attic* (New York: HarperCollins Children's Books, 1981), 90.

33. Makoto Fujimura, *Culture Care: Reconnecting with Beauty for Our Common Life* (Downers Grove: InterVarsity Press, 2017), 55–56.

34. Coates, "Hope and the Artist."

35. Revelation 21:1–5.

36. J. R. R. Tolkien, "On Fairy-Stories," in *Tree and Leaf* (London: HarperCollins, 2001), 68–69.

37. Hopkins, "God's Grandeur," in *Poems and Prose*, 27.

38. N. T. Wright, *Surprised by Hope: Rethinking Heaven, the Resurrection, and the Mission of the Church* (New York: HarperOne, 2008), 102.

39. "Here I lift my Ebenezer; Hither by thy help I'm come" is a line from Robert Robinson, "Come, Thou Fount of Every Blessing" (1758).

40. Luke 12:27–28.

41. Job 38:4.

42. Job 38:12.

43. Clarkson, *This Beautiful Truth*, 37–38.

CHAPTER 6

1. This distinction is similar to Svendsen's distinction between situational and existential boredom. Lars Svendsen, *A Philosophy of Boredom*, trans. John Irons (London: Reaktion Books, 2005), 42–43.

2. Richard Beck, *Hunting Magic Eels: Recovering an Enchanted Faith in a Skeptical Age* (Minneapolis: Broadleaf Books, 2021), 95.

3. For example, see Guihyun Park, Beng-Cong Lim, and Hui Si Oh, "Why Being Bored Might Not Be a Bad Thing After All," in *Academy of Management Discoveries* 5, no 1. (March 26, 2019), https://journals.aom.org/doi/10.5465/amd.2017.0033.

4. Søren Kierkegaard, *Either/Or: A Fragment of Life*, trans. Alastair Hannay (New York: Penguin, 1992), 230.

5. Walker Percy, *Lost in the Cosmos: The Last Self-Help Book* (New York: Picador, 1983), 70–71.

6. 1 Kings 17:7–16.

7. *The Office*, season 2, episode 3, "Office Olympics," October 4, 2005. In this case, office boredom led to the creation of office Olympics, so this may be an example of "productive" boredom as discussed above, even though it produced more fun instead of more work.

8. Georges Bernanos, *The Diary of a Country Priest*, trans. Pamela Morris (1937; repr., Philadelphia: Da Capo Press, 2022), 2.

9. Blaise Pascal, *Pensées* (New York: Penguin, 1995), 40.

10. David Brooks writes about "the Achievatron" as it relates to the cycle of child-raising, schooling, career advancement, and upward mobility, and a similar cycle is evident in a busy approach to spiritual life. David Brooks, *On Paradise Drive: How We Live Now (and Always Have) in the Future Tense* (New York: Simon and Schuster, 2004), 142ff.

11. Andrew Root, *The Congregation in a Secular Age: Keeping Sacred Time against the Speed of Modern Life* (Grand Rapids: Baker Academic, 2021), 32–33.

12. Andrew Root discusses this campaign as an example of what we deem necessary for alleviating our boredom and alienation. Root, *Congregation in a Secular Age*, 182.

13. Psalm 5:3.

14. Psalm 27:13–14.

15. Psalm 130:5–6; Romans 8:23–25.

16. 1 Thessalonians 1:10; Titus 2:13; James 5:7.

17. Isaiah 65:17; 2 Peter 3:13.

18. Romans 8:18–19.

19. Andrew Root, *Churches and the Crisis of Decline: A Hopeful, Practical Ecclesiology for a Secular Age* (Grand Rapids: Baker Academic, 2022), 161.

20. This is not the space to debate the ethics of hunting and

whether this is a beautiful or ugly act, but for me and my family, hunting has always been an act of conservation, a source for sustainable and healthy food, and a respectful expression of our role within the community of creation.

21. Beckett, *Waiting for Godot*, 109.

22. Svendsen, *A Philosophy of Boredom*, 140.

23. Svendsen, *A Philosophy of Boredom*, 47–48.

24. Svendsen, *A Philosophy of Boredom*, 154.

25. Root, *Churches and the Crisis of Decline*, 33.

26. Chesterton, *Orthodoxy*, 108–9.

27. Simone Weil, *Gravity and Grace*, trans. Arthur Wills (1952; repr., Lincoln: Bison Books, 1997), 233.

28. Wendell Berry, *A Timbered Choir: The Sabbath Poems 1979–1997* (Washington, DC: Counterpoint, 1999), 209.

29. For more on slowness in contrast to fast-life values, see Carl Honore, *In Praise of Slowness: Challenging the Cult of Speed* (New York: HarperOne, 2005).

30. Hartmut Rosa, *Alienation and Acceleration: Towards a Critical Theory of Late-Modern Temporality* (Aarhus: Aarhus University Press, 2010).

31. Hartmut Rosa, *Resonance: A Sociology of Our Relationship to the World*, trans. James C. Wagner (Cambridge, MA: Polity Press, 2019), 179.

32. The paragraph that follows is a summary of Capon, *Supper of the Lamb*, 10–17.

33. Rosa calls these resonant relationships "energetically charged forms of contact." Rosa, *Resonance*, 137.

34. Dillard, *Pilgrim at Tinker Creek*, 271.

35. Steven Bouma-Prediger, *Earthkeeping and Character: Exploring a Christian Ecological Virtue Ethic* (Grand Rapids: Baker Academic, 2020), 44.

36. I'm influenced here by Eugene Peterson's vision for the

"unbusy pastor" in Eugene H. Peterson, *The Contemplative Pastor: Returning to the Art of Spiritual Direction* (Grand Rapids: Eerdmans, 1989).

37. Mary Oliver, "Messenger," in *Thirst* (Boston: Beacon, 2006), 1.

CHAPTER 7

1. Sam Wells writes about the significance of Jesus's Nazareth years and how this mode of "being with" is the essence of the gospel. Sam Wells, *A Nazareth Manifesto: Being with God* (Oxford: Wiley-Blackwell, 2015).

2. Jonathan Edwards, *The Works of Jonathan Edwards*, ed. George S. Claghorn, vol. 16, *Letters and Personal Writings* (New Haven: Yale University Press, 1998), 163–64. Edwards was one of the preeminent theologians of beauty, and you can read more about his theology of beauty in Owen Strachen and Doug Sweeney, *Jonathan Edwards on Beauty*, The Essential Edwards Collection (Chicago: Moody Publishers, 2010).

3. Mary Oliver, "Mindful," in *New and Selected Poems: Volume Two* (Boston: Beacon, 2005), 90.

4. Jon Acuff, *Stuff Christians Like* (Grand Rapids: Zondervan, 2020). Acuff does not specifically discuss "radical" in his book, but he humorously engages similar ideas.

5. Despite my reticence about the word "radical," this is what David Platt wants to emphasize in his book *Radical: Taking Back Your Faith from the American Dream* (Colorado Springs: Multnomah, 2010).

6. This is John Stott's explanation for using *radical* in the title of his book *The Radical Disciple*, which is a great book. Unfortunately, beauty is not one of the topics that Stott highlights as neglected

aspects of our Christian calling. John Stott, *The Radical Disciple: Some Neglected Aspects of Our Calling* (Downers Grove: IVP, 2012).

7. Along these lines, I appreciate Michael Horton's book *Ordinary: Sustainable Faith in a Radical, Restless World* (Grand Rapids: Zondervan, 2014).

8. Colossians 1:17; Hebrews 1:3.

9. O'Donohue, *Beauty*, 28.

10. Rachel Carson, *The Sense of Wonder: A Celebration of Nature for Parents and Children* (1965; repr., New York: Harper Perennial, 2017), 44.

11. Timothy D. Willard, *The Beauty Chasers: Recapturing the Wonder of the Divine* (Grand Rapids: Zondervan, 2022).

12. Sarah Ruhl, *100 Essays I Don't Have Time to Write: On Umbrellas and Sword Fights, Parades and Dogs, Fire Alarms, Children, and Theatre* (New York: Farrar, Straus and Giroux, 2014), 215.

13. Manifesto of the Cloud Appreciation Society, https://cloudappreciationsociety.org/manifesto, accessed January 11, 2023.

14. Fabiana Fondevila, *Where Wonder Lives: Practices for Cultivating the Sacred in Your Daily Life*, trans. Nick Inman (Rochester, VT: Findhorn Press, 2021), 60.

15. Lewis's seven-volume *The Chronicles of Narnia* was published 1950–1956, and his space trilogy was published 1938–1945; George MacDonald, *At the Back of the North Wind* (London: Strahan & Co., 1871); Wilson Rawls, *Where the Red Fern Grows* (New York: Doubleday, 1961); Alan Paton, *Cry, the Beloved Country* (London: Jonathan Cape, 1949).

16. J. R. R. Tolkien, *Tree and Leaf*, 63. Tolkien makes fine distinctions between fantasy, myth, and fairy tales, but I have lumped them together by virtue of their similarities.

17. Tolkien, *Tree and Leaf*, 58.

18. Willard, *The Beauty Chasers*, 202.

19. O'Donohue, *Beauty*, 13.

20. Norman Wirzba, *Living the Sabbath: Discovering the Rhythms of Rest and Delight* (Grand Rapids: Brazos, 2006), 53.

21. Dan Allender, *Sabbath* (Nashville: Thomas Nelson, 2009), 67.

22. C. S. Lewis, *Reflections on the Psalms* (1958; repr., New York: HarperOne, 2017), 111.

23. W. David O. Taylor, *Glimpses of the New Creation: Worship and the Formative Power of the Arts* (Grand Rapids: Eerdmans, 2019), 245.

24. Hebrews 10:23–25.

25. Alejandro García-Rivera, *The Community of the Beautiful: A Theological Aesthetics* (Collegeville, MN: Liturgical Press, 1999), 195.

26. Andy Crouch, *Culture Making: Recovering Our Creative Calling* (Downers Grove: InterVarsity Press, 2013).

27. Sub-creation is Tolkien's word for our image-bearing capacity to create, not *ex nihilo* like God, but refracting the white light of God's creativity into beautiful hues. Tolkien, *Tree and Leaf*, 56.

28. Clarkson, *This Beautiful Truth*, 182, 188.

29. Madeleine L'Engle, *Walking on Water: Reflections on Faith and Art* (New York: Convergent Books, 2016), 98.

30. 1 Corinthians 10:31.

31. I'm borrowing this phrase from Francis Schaeffer, *No Little People*, rev. ed. (Wheaton: Crossway, 2021).

32. Following the unknown, spurious quote by Martin Luther: "If I knew the world were ending tomorrow, I would plant an apple tree today."

33. Wendell Berry, "Manifesto: Mad Farmer's Liberation Front," in *New Collected Poems* (Berkeley: Counterpoint, 2012).

34. Carroll, "How to Prepare for the Second Coming," in *Habitation of Wonder*, 106.

35. Annie Dillard, *The Writing Life* (1989; repr., New York: Harper Perennial, 2013), 32.

CHAPTER 8

1. Fyodor Dostoevsky, *The Idiot*, trans. Anna Brailovsky and Constance Garnett (New York: Random House, 2003), 415. For more on beauty as a riddle, see Fyodor Dostoevsky, *The Brothers Karamazov*, trans. Constance Garnett (New York: Modern Library, 1996), 117. Cf. Dostoevsky, *The Idiot*, 82.

2. Mary Oliver, interview by Krista Tippett, *On Being*, Public Radio Exchange, February 5, 2015.

3. Riley, *This Here Flesh*, 40.

4. Jason Goroncy, "Daring Imagination," in *Imagination in an Age of Crisis: Soundings from the Arts and Theology*, ed. Jason Goroncy and Rod Patterson (Eugene: Wipf & Stock, 2022), 1.

5. Goroncy, "Daring Imagination," 4. He contrasts this approach to the proposal of philosopher and cultural critic Santiago Zabala in *Why Only Art Can Save Us: Aesthetics and the Absence of Emergency* (New York: Columbia University Press, 2017).

6. Erica Jong, "Picking Up My Pen Again," in *At the Edge of the Body* (New York: Holt, Rinehart and Winston, 1979), 35.

7. Gregory Wolfe, *Beauty Will Save the World: Recovering the Human in an Ideological Age* (Wilmington, DE: Intercollegiate Studies Institute, 2011), 33.

8. See the chapter on beauty in N. T. Wright, *Broken Signposts: How Christianity Makes Sense of the World* (New York: HarperOne, 2020).

9. Lewis, "The Weight of Glory."

10. Chris Green, *All Things Beautiful: An Aesthetic Christology* (Waco: Baylor University Press, 2021), 87.

11. This is similar to Karl Barth's way of speaking about the triune God as Revealer (Father), Revelation (Son), and Revealedness (Spirit). Karl Barth, *Church Dogmatics*, vol. I/1, ed. Geoffrey W. Bromiley and T. F. Torrance, trans. Geoffrey W. Bromiley (Edinburgh: T&T Clark, 1936), 295.

12. Brian Zhand unpacks the notion of "cruciform beauty" in *Beauty Will Save the World: Rediscovering the Allure and Mystery of Christianity* (Lake Mary, FL: Charisma House, 2012).

13. 1 Corinthians 1:18.

14. Green, *All Things Beautiful*, 87. Or as Jimmy Myers puts it, "you can only be saved by the beautiful one who has become the ugly one." Jimmy Myers, "Is It True that 'The World Will Be Saved by Beauty'?" *First Things*, July 17, 2015, https://www.firstthings.com/web-exclusives/2015/07/student-essay-contest-winner-first-place.

15. Romans 6:8–9.

16. Bruno Forte, *The Portal of Beauty: Towards a Theological Aesthetics* (Grand Rapids: Eerdmans, 2008), 118.

17. Helen Howarth Lemmel, "Turn Your Eyes Upon Jesus," 1922.

18. Dana Gioia, "The Catholic Writer Today," *First Things*, December 2013, https://www.firstthings.com/article/2013/12/the-catholic-writer-today.

19. Romans 10:12–15; cf. Isaiah 52:7.

20. Psalm 19:1; Romans 1:20.

21. Ephesians 1:10.

22. For an excellent assessment of the Spirit's connection to created beauty, see W. David O. Taylor, "Spirit and Beauty: A Reappraisal," *Christian Scholars Review* 44, no. 1 (2014): 45–59. He concludes: "The Spirit . . . instantiates, illumines, communicates, and completes [the beauty of God] through the created realm."

23. See David Bentley Hart, *Theological Territories: A David Bentley Hart Digest* (Notre Dame: University of Notre Dame Press, 2020), which has an excellent chapter on beauty as the pouring out and emptying (kenosis) of divine being.

24. Dillard, *Pilgrim at Tinker Creek*, 148.

25. Romans 8:21.

26. Romans 8:22–25.

27. Czeslaw Milosz, "One More Day," in *New and Collected Poems 1931–2001* (New York: HarperCollins, 2001).

28. Song of Songs 8:6–7.

29. Patitsas, *The Ethics of Beauty*, 619.

30. Revelation 21:5.

ACKNOWLEDGMENTS

1. Dillard, *The Writing Life*, 72.

Select Bibliography

Akomolafe, Bayo. *These Wilds Beyond Our Fences: Letters to My Daughter on Humanity's Search for Home.* Berkeley: North Atlantic Books, 2017.

Alexander, Kathryn B. *Saving Beauty: A Theological Aesthetics of Nature.* Minneapolis: Fortress Press, 2014.

Allender, Dan. *Sabbath.* Nashville: Thomas Nelson, 2009.

Augustine. *Confessions.* Translated by Henry Chadwick. Oxford: Oxford University Press, 1991.

Balthasar, Hans Urs von. *The Glory of the Lord: A Theological Aesthetics*, vol. 1, *Seeing the Form.* Translated by Erasmo Leiva-Merikakis. Edinburgh: T&T Clark, 1992.

Barth, Karl. *Church Dogmatics.* Volume I/1. Translated by G. W. Bromiley. Edited by Geoffrey W. Bromiley and T. F. Torrance. Edinburgh: T&T Clark, 1936.

———. *Church Dogmatics.* Volume II/2. Translated by G. W. Bromiley et al. Edited by Geoffrey W. Bromiley and T. F. Torrance. Edinburgh: T&T Clark, 1957.

Beck, Richard. *Hunting Magic Eels: Recovering an Enchanted Faith in a Skeptical Age.* Minneapolis: Broadleaf Books, 2021.

Beckett, Samuel. *Waiting for Godot: A Tragicomedy in Two Acts*. New York: Grove Press, 2011.

Begbie, Jeremy. *A Peculiar Orthodoxy: Reflections on Theology and the Arts*. Grand Rapids: Baker Academic, 2018.

———. *Redeeming Transcendence in the Arts: Bearing Witness to the Triune God*. Grand Rapids: Eerdmans, 2018.

———. *Resounding Truth: Christian Wisdom in a World of Music*. Grand Rapids: Baker Academic, 2007.

Begbie, Jeremy, Daniel Train, and W. David O. Taylor, eds. *The Art of New Creation: Trajectories in Theology and the Arts*. Downers Grove: IVP Academic, 2022.

Bernanos, Georges. *The Diary of a Country Priest*. Translated by Pamela Morris. Philadelphia: Da Capo Press, 2022.

Berry, Wendell. *New Collected Poems*. Berkeley: Counterpoint, 2012.

———. *A Timbered Choir: The Sabbath Poems 1979–1997*. Washington, DC: Counterpoint, 1999.

Bouma-Prediger, Steven. *Earthkeeping and Character: Exploring a Christian Ecological Virtue Ethic*. Grand Rapids: Baker Academic, 2020.

Buechner, Frederick. *The Remarkable Ordinary*. Grand Rapids: Zondervan, 2017.

Capon, Robert Farrar. *The Supper of the Lamb: A Culinary Reflection*. New York: Modern Library, 2002.

Carnes, Natalie. *Beauty: A Theological Engagement with Gregory of Nyssa*. Eugene: Cascade, 2014.

Carroll, Abigail. *Habitation of Wonder*. Eugene: Cascade, 2018.

Carson, Rachel. *The Sense of Wonder: A Celebration of Nature for Parents and Children*. New York: Harper Perennial, 2017.

Chesterton, G. K. *Orthodoxy*. New York: Doubleday, 2001.

Select Bibliography

Clarkson, Sarah. *This Beautiful Truth: How God's Goodness Breaks into Our Darkness*. Grand Rapids: Baker, 2021.

Coates, Ta-Nehisi. *Between the World and Me*. New York: Spiegel and Grau, 2015.

———. "Hope and the Artist: The Virtues of Enlightenment over Feel-Goodism." *The Atlantic*, November 23, 2015.

Crawford, Matthew B. *The World beyond Your Head: On Becoming an Individual in an Age of Distraction*. New York: Farrar, Straus and Giroux, 2016.

Crouch, Andy. *Culture Making: Recovering Our Creative Calling*. Downers Grove: InterVarsity Press, 2013.

Danto, Arthur. *The Abuse of Beauty: Aesthetics and the Concept of Art*. Chicago: Open Court, 2003.

Desmond, William. *The Gift of Beauty and the Passion of Being: On the Threshold between the Aesthetic and the Religious*. Eugene: Cascade, 2018.

Dickinson, Emily. *The Complete Poems of Emily Dickinson*. Edited by Thomas H. Johnson. New York: Back Bay Books, 1976.

Dillard, Annie. *Pilgrim at Tinker Creek*. New York: Harper Perennial, 1998.

———. *The Writing Life*. New York: Harper Perennial, 2013.

Dostoevsky, Fyodor. *The Brothers Karamazov*. Translated by Constance Garnett. New York: Modern Library, 1996.

———. *The Idiot*. Translated by Anna Brailovsky and Constance Garnett. New York: Random House, 2003.

Doyle, Brian. *How the Light Gets In and Other Headlong Epiphanies*. Maryknoll, NY: Orbis, 2015.

Edwards, Jonathan. *Letters and Personal Writings*. Edited by George S. Claghorn. *The Works of Jonathan Edwards*, vol. 16. New Haven: Yale University Press, 1998.

Emerson, Ralph Waldo. *Nature and Selected Essays*. New York: Penguin, 2003.

Farley, Wendy. *Beguiled by Beauty: Cultivating a Life of Contemplation and Compassion*. Louisville: Westminster John Knox Press, 2020.

Forte, Bruno. *The Portal of Beauty: Towards a Theological Aesthetics*. Grand Rapids: Eerdmans, 2008.

Fujimura, Makoto. *Art and Faith: A Theology of Making*. New Haven: Yale University Press, 2020.

———. *Culture Care: Reconnecting with Beauty for Our Common Life*. Downers Grove: InterVarsity Press, 2017.

———. *Silence and Beauty: Hidden Faith Born of Suffering*. Downers Grove: InterVarsity Press, 2016.

García-Rivera, Alejandro. *The Community of the Beautiful: A Theological Aesthetics*. Collegeville, MN: The Liturgical Press, 1999.

Gay, Ross. *The Book of Delights*. Chapel Hill: Workmans' Publishing, 2019.

Gioia, Dana. "The Catholic Writer Today." *First Things*. December 2013. https://www.firstthings.com/article/2013/12/the-catholic-writer-today.

Goroncy, Jason, and Rod Patterson, eds. *Imagination in an Age of Crisis: Soundings from the Arts and Theology*. Eugene: Wipf & Stock, 2022.

Green, Chris. *All Things Beautiful: An Aesthetic Christology*. Waco: Baylor University Press, 2021.

Gruchy, John W. de. *Christianity, Art, and Transformation: Theological Aesthetics in the Struggle for Justice*. Cambridge: Cambridge University Press, 2001.

Guthrie, Steven R. *Creator Spirit: The Holy Spirit and the Art of Becoming Human*. Grand Rapids: Baker, 2011.

Hart, David Bentley. *The Beauty of the Infinite: The Aesthetics of Christian Truth*. Grand Rapids: Eerdmans, 2013.

———. *The Experience of God: Being, Consciousness, Bliss*. New Haven: Yale University Press, 2013.

Hartse, Joel Heng. *Dancing about Architecture Is a Reasonable Thing to Do: Writing about Music, Meaning, and the Ineffable*. Eugene: Cascade, 2022.

Hildebrand, Dietrich von. *Aesthetics*, vol. 1. Translated by Hildebrand Project. Steubenville, OH: Hildebrand Project, 2016.

———. *Beauty in the Light of Redemption*. Steubenville, OH: Hildebrand Press, 2019.

Honore, Carl. *In Praise of Slowness: Challenging the Cult of Speed*. New York: HarperOne, 2005.

Hopkins, Gerard Manley. *Poems and Prose*. New York: Penguin, 1953.

Jennings, Willie James. *The Christian Imagination: Theology and the Origins of Race*. New Haven: Yale University Press, 2010.

Keillor, Garrison. *Lake Wobegon Days*. New York: Viking, 1985.

Kierkegaard, Soren. *Either/Or: A Fragment of Life*. Translated by Alastair Hannay. New York: Penguin, 1992.

Kilby, Clyde. *The Arts and Christian Imagination: Essays on Art, Literature, and Aesthetics*. Brewster, MA: Paraclete Press, 2016.

Kolk, Bessel A. van der. *The Body Keeps Score: Brain, Mind, and Body in the Healing of Trauma*. New York: Penguin, 2015.

Lane, Belden C. *Ravished by Beauty: The Surprising Legacy of the Reformed Tradition*. Oxford: Oxford University Press, 2011.

L'Engle, Madeleine. *Walking on Water: Reflections on Faith and Art*. New York: Convergent Books, 2016.

Lewis, C. S. *The Collected Letters of C. S. Lewis*, vol. 1. Edited by Walter Hooper. San Francisco: HarperCollins, 2004.

———. *An Experiment in Criticism*. Cambridge: Cambridge University Press, 2012.

———. *The Lion, the Witch and the Wardrobe*. New York: HarperCollins, 1950.

———. *Reflections on the Psalms*. New York: HarperOne, 2017.

———. *The Weight of Glory*. New York: HarperOne, 2001.

McCampbell, Mary W. *Imagining Our Neighbors as Ourselves: How Art Shapes Empathy*. Minneapolis: Fortress Press, 2022.

Milosz, Czeslaw. *New and Collected Poems 1931–2001*. New York: HarperCollins, 2001.

Nestor, James. *Breath: The New Science of a Lost Art*. New York: Riverhead Books, 2021.

Noble, Alan. *Disruptive Witness: Speaking Truth in a Distracted Age*. Downers Grove: InterVarsity Press, 2018.

O'Connor, Flannery. *A Prayer Journal*. New York: Farrar, Straus and Giroux, 2013.

O'Donohue, John. *Beauty: The Invisible Embrace*. New York: HarperCollins, 2004.

Oliver, Mary. *New and Selected Poems: Volume Two*. Boston: Beacon Press, 2005.

———. *Thirst*. Boston: Beacon Press, 2006.

———. *Upstream: Selected Essays*. New York: Penguin, 2019.

Orang, Bahar. *Where Things Touch: A Meditation on Beauty*. Toronto: Book*hug Press, 2020.

Pascal, Blaise. *Pensées*. New York: Penguin, 1995.

Patitsas, Timothy. *The Ethics of Beauty*. Maysville, MO: St Nicholas Press, 2020.

Percy, Walker. *Lost in the Cosmos: The Last Self-Help Book*. New York: Picador, 1983.

Peterson, Eugene. *The Contemplative Pastor: Returning to the Art of Spiritual Direction*. Grand Rapids: Eerdmans, 1989.

———. *Under the Unpredictable Plant: An Exploration in Vocational Holiness.* Grand Rapids: Eerdmans, 1992.

Pseudo-Dionysius the Areopagite. *The Divine Names; The Mystical Theology.* Translated by John D. Jones. Milwaukee: Marquette University Press, 1980.

Riley, Cole Arthur. *This Here Flesh: Spirituality, Liberation, and the Stories that Make Us.* New York: Convergent Books, 2022.

Rookmaaker, Hans. *Art Needs No Justification.* Vancouver: Regent College Publishing, 2010.

Rooney, Sally. *Beautiful World, Where Are You?* New York: Farrar, Straus and Giroux, 2021.

Root, Andrew. *Churches and the Crisis of Decline: A Hopeful, Practical Ecclesiology for a Secular Age.* Grand Rapids: Baker Academic, 2022.

———. *The Congregation in a Secular Age: Keeping Sacred Time against the Speed of Modern Life.* Grand Rapids: Baker Academic, 2021.

———. *The Pastor in a Secular Age: Ministry to People Who No Longer Need a God.* Grand Rapids: Baker Academic, 2019.

Rosa, Hartmut. *Resonance: A Sociology of Our Relationship with the World.* Translated by James C. Wagner. Medford, MA: Polity Press, 2019.

Ruhl, Sarah. *100 Essays I Don't Have Time to Write: On Umbrellas and Sword Fights, Parades and Dogs, Fire Alarms, Children, and Theatre.* New York: Farrar, Straus and Giroux, 2014.

Sammon, Brendan Thomas. *Called to Attraction: An Introduction to the Theology of Beauty.* Eugene: Cascade, 2017.

Scarry, Elaine. *On Beauty and Being Just.* Princeton: Princeton University Press, 1999.

Schleske, Martin. *The Sound of Life's Unspeakable Beauty.* Translated by Janet Leigh Gesme. Grand Rapids: Eerdmans, 2020.

Scruton, Roger. *Beauty: A Very Short Introduction*. Oxford: Oxford University Press, 2011.

Seerveld, Calvin. *A Christian Critique of Art and Literature*. Sioux Center: Dordt College Press, 1995.

———. *Rainbows for a Fallen World*. Toronto: Toronto Tuppence Press, 1980.

Silverstein, Shel. *A Light in the Attic*. New York: HarperCollins Children's Books, 1981.

Strachen, Owen, and Doug Sweeney. *Jonathan Edwards on Beauty*. The Essential Edwards Collection. Chicago: Moody Publishers, 2010.

Svendsen, Lars. *A Philosophy of Boredom*. Translated by John Irons. London: Reaktion Books, 2005.

Taylor, Charles. *A Secular Age*. Cambridge: Belknap Press, 2007.

Taylor, W. David O. *Glimpses of the New Creation: Worship and the Formative Power of the Arts*. Grand Rapids: Eerdmans, 2019.

———. "Spirit and Beauty: A Reappraisal." *Christian Scholars Review* 44, no. 1 (2014): 45–59.

Tolkien, J. R. R. *Tree and Leaf*. London: HarperCollins, 2001.

Treir, Daniel, Mark Husbands, and Roger Lundin, eds. *The Beauty of God: Theology and the Arts*. Downers Grove: InterVarsity Press, 2007.

Vander Lugt, Wesley. *Living Theodrama: Reimagining Theological Ethics*. London: Routledge, 2014.

Weil, Simone. *Gravity and Grace*. Translated by Arthur Wills. Lincoln, NE: Bison Books, 1997.

Wells, Samuel. *A Nazareth Manifesto: Being with God*. Oxford: Wiley-Blackwell, 2015.

———. *Walk Humbly: Encouragements for Living, Working, and Being*. Grand Rapids: Eerdmans, 2019.

Willard, Timothy D. *The Beauty Chasers: Recapturing the Wonder of the Divine*. Grand Rapids: Zondervan, 2022.

Williams, Terry Tempest. *Erosion*. New York: Sarah Crichton Books, 2019.

Williams, William Carlos. *Asphodel, That Greeny Flower & Other Love Poems*. New York: New Directions Books, 1994.

Wiman, Christian. *Every Riven Thing*. New York: Farrar, Straus and Giroux, 2011.

———. *My Bright Abyss: Meditation of a Modern Believer*. New York: Farrar, Straus and Giroux, 2013.

Wirzba, Norman. *Living the Sabbath: Discovering the Rhythms of Rest and Delight*. Grand Rapids: Brazos, 2006.

———. *This Sacred Life: Humanity's Place in a Wounded World*. Cambridge: Cambridge University Press, 2021.

Wolfe, Gregory. *Beauty Will Save the World: Recovering the Human in an Ideological Age*. Wilmington, DE: Intercollegiate Studies Institute, 2011.

Wolterstorff, Nicholas. *Art Rethought: The Social Practices of Art*. Oxford: Oxford University Press, 2015.

Wright, N. T. *Broken Signposts: How Christianity Makes Sense of the World*. New York: HarperOne, 2020.

———. *Surprised by Hope: Rethinking Heaven, the Resurrection, and the Mission of the Church*. New York: HarperOne, 2008.

Zhand, Brian. *Beauty Will Save the World: Rediscovering the Allure and Mystery of Christianity*. Lake Mary, FL: Charisma House, 2012.

Name and Subject Index

creation, beauty of, 20, 22–24,
50, 84–85, 108, 118, 123–24,
133–34, 135; and environmen-
tal/climate crisis, 29, 70–71,
72, 73–74, 136; extravagance
and profuse variety of, 22–24,
72–74, 146n22; forests and
woods, 3, 40–41, 72, 84, 92,
100, 108, 110, 123–24, 135;
joyful beauty, 90–92, 102;
repetition/monotony in, 102
creativity and human artistry,
76, 85–86, 91–92, 96, 101–2,
119–20, 129, 137, 138. *See also*
artistic beauty
"cross pressure," 32–33, 36, 37, 49
crucifixion, of Jesus, 7, 53, 65,
126, 131
Crusades, 62
Cry, the Beloved Country (Paton), 55, 114

Daniele da Volterra, 61
Danto, Arthur, 143n2
decentering, 43–45, 57,
149–50n15
*Desiring God: Meditations of a
Christian Hedonist* (Piper), 80
Desmond, William, 2, 32
Dickinson, Emily, 82
Dillard, Annie, 2, 4, 106, 121,
129–30, 149n28
Dinesen, Isak, 77
disponibility (availability),
cultivating, 46

Dostoevsky, Fyodor, 19, 122,
152n55
Dove, Rita, 17
Doyle, Brian, 21

"Ebenezer collage," 91–92, 136
Ecclesiastes, beauty-centric
commands of, 78, 80, 81
Edwards, Jonathan, 108, 162n2
Emerson, Ralph Waldo, 19, 48
empathy, 54–57
entanglement, and beauty, 3,
6–7, 40, 50, 53–54, 57–58,
63–64, 67, 81

fairy tales, 29, 89–90, 114–15, 136
Farago, Jason, 71
Farley, Wendy, 20, 44, 85
Father John Misty (musician),
94–95
Floor Is Lava (TV show), 158n30
Floyd, George, 62, 76
Fondevila, Fabiana, 113
forest bathing (*shinrin-yoku*),
40–41, 135
forests and woods, 3, 40–41, 72,
84, 92, 100, 108, 110, 123–24,
135
Forte, Bruno, 126
Francis, Pope, 73
Franklin, Aretha, 41
Friends (TV show), 29
Fujimura, Makoto, 54, 66, 89

García-Rivera, Alejandro, 118
Garner, Eric, 62
Gast, John, 61

60–65, 74, 135; police violence against Black Americans, 62, 76

radical faith, 108–9, 162n5, 162n6

Rawls, Wilson, 114

Rent (musical), 55

repentance, 37–38, 121, 134

resurrection, Jesus's and ours, 68, 117, 120, 125–26

Rexha, Bebe, 32

Riley, Cole Arthur, 87, 123

Rooney, Sally, 61

Root, Andrew, 30, 98, 99

Rosa, Harmut, 103–4, 105

Ruhl, Sarah, 111

Sabbath, 115–16, 138

Saint Patrick's Breastplate prayer, 58, 153n67

Sallman, Warner, 61

Sammon, Brendan Thomas, 151n31

Scarry, Elaine, 43

Schaeffer, Francis, 164n31

Schleske, Martin, 54

Schumacher, Sara, 73–74

Scream, The (Munch painting), 82

Scruton, Roger, 143n3

Seerveld, Calvin, 6, 67, 150n26

sentimentality, 66–68, 70, 85

Silverstein, Shel, 88

Simpsons, The (TV show), 30–31

slicing an onion (practice of), 104–5, 137

Smailovic, Vedran, 86

Smith, James K. A., 6

social media and online entertainment, 5, 49, 68

solas, Reformational, 131

Solnit, Rebecca, 149–50n15

soul, 12–17, 133; *nephesh* (Hebrew), 12–13; *psychē/psyche* (Greek/English), 14. *See also* buffered souls; porous souls

Soul (2020 film), 15

Springsteen, Bruce, 94

stargazing, 47–49, 135

Stinky & Dirty Show, The (animated TV show), 87

Stott, John, 162n6

sublime, 6–7, 144n13

Svendsen, Lars, 101, 159n1

Taylor, Charles, 4, 29, 31, 32, 48, 49, 147n1

Taylor, W. David O., 117, 166n22

"Terreauty" ("terrible beauty"), 65–66, 155n16

terror and beauty, 65–67, 68, 135, 155n16

Thin Red Line, The (1998 film), 55

Third Reich, 61

This Beautiful Truth (Clarkson), 86, 93, 119

Thomas Aquinas, 144n7

times of crisis, beauty in, 5, 26, 76–79, 81–87, 91–93, 124–25

Tippett, Krista, 123

Scripture Index

Scripture Index